Michelle,

THANKS for laughing, keep pushing. unpushed.

**YOUR
COUNTRY
IS JUST NOT
THAT INTO
YOU**

YOUR COUNTRY IS JUST **NOT** THAT INTO YOU

How the Media, Wall Street,
and Both Political Parties
Keep on Screwing You—
Even After You've Moved On

JIMMY DORE

RUNNING PRESS
PHILADELPHIA · LONDON

Published by Running Press,
A Member of the Perseus Books Group

Books published by Running Press are available at special discounts for bulk purchases in the United States by corporations, institutions, and other organizations. For more information, please contact the Special Markets Department at the Perseus Books Group, 2300 Chestnut Street, Suite 200, Philadelphia, PA 19103, or call (800) 810-4145, ext. 5000, or e-mail special.markets@perseusbooks.com.

ISBN 978-0-7624-5351-1
Library of Congress Control Number: 2014937554

E-book ISBN 978-0-7624-5352-8

9   8   7   6   5   4   3   2   1
Digit on the right indicates the number of this printing

Designed by Bill Jones
Edited by Jennifer Kasius
Typography: Stone Sans, Stone Serif, Stone Informal, and Univers

Running Press Book Publishers
2300 Chestnut Street
Philadelphia, PA 19103-4371

Visit us on the web!
www.runningpress.com

CONTENTS

THE SERIOUS BIT AT THE BEGINNING

I don't know if this is a foreword, a preface, or an introduction (my appendix is already removed). For years as a comedian, I only watched television news to keep up with current events. At the beginning of my career, my comedy was not very concerned with politics.

That all changed with the Iraq war. The lies of government and the lazy complicity of the media made me realize that politics has consequences. After countless nights of throwing shoes at my television, I ran out of shoes and looked for alternatives, but throwing televisions at my shoes hurt my back.

Realizing the problems facing America are too important not to make fun of, I started bringing my views on stage with me. I've been a professional comedian my entire life, but I'm really just a member of the public. In my Comedy Central specials, media appearances, and radio shows, I have tried to put the "public" back into the "public discourse." The mainstream media serves power instead of questioning it—the incestuous beltway punditocracy talks to itself, trying to curry favor or maintain "access"—indulging in a discourse completely divorced from the lives and realities of working Americans.

TV news has become a haven for careerists and opportunists. When the economy collapsed, the supposed business "experts" didn't know what hit them. After the wars in the Middle East dragged on, there was no Hall of Shame for the pundits that got it wrong—they never had to face disgrace while American soldiers faced bullets. The talking heads that engage in the most odious race-baiting are rewarded with promotions and more air time. These same think-tank Mediaocrities continue to contaminate the news cycles, calling for the persecution of patriots like Snowden and Manning, just as they derided the people who opposed the Iraq war a decade ago.

Watch the commercials for the Sunday morning shows, and

you'll see that they're sponsored by your friendly local military contractor. I don't know about you, but I don't plan on purchasing a
747 anytime soon . . . so why does Boeing buy airtime every Sunday?

CNN seems designed for necrophiliacs. Fox News panders to the
demographic that needs their prejudices confirmed (you'd think
Fox News would support universal healthcare just to keep their geri-
atric audience alive). It's called "old media" for a reason. No wonder
viewers are leaving network news in droves. Young people are finding
alternatives on the Internet, where voices can be uncensored and
more honest.

It's easy to fixate on Fox News—the Lee Atwater wet-dream network (the Southern Strategy made national)—but they're only part
of the problem. You can imagine the Hannitys and O'Reillys cashing
their monthly million-dollar checks with the rationalization that,
instead of giving the public what it needs, they give it what it wants.
Sadly, they still successfully pollute the public's perception of important issues. Bush lied us into a war, Obama lied us into healthcare—
which one are you more upset by?

The media is only one facet of the deeper problem in America.
That problem is money in politics. Our elected officials serve money
and not the people. This is not because all of them are inherently
corrupt, but because our political system has been retrofitted to
accommodate the interests of the wealthy. Politicians give lip service
to issues like inequality and then give actual lip service to the corporations responsible for it (the hooker behind the liquor store type of
lip service). The two parties are conglomerated with moneyed interests as election campaigns have become open markets of legal
bribery. The most loyal corporate soldiers are rewarded with lobbying
or consultant jobs after serving their time in political office.

This is money without nationality or loyalty or empathy—and it
has the loudest voice in our country. The ultimate aim of American
politics today is figuring out how the wealthy can persuade the most

amount of people to use their vote to keep wealth in power. Of course, society's struggle against concentrations of power is eternal. But we are far away from the era of trust-busting and the New Deal that gave working Americans a say in the future for them and their families. Today the pendulum has swung dangerously far with little sign of it swinging back.

Don't think it's all doom and gloom. In America, the people are better than their politicians, and with social issues, the public is far ahead of its supposed representatives. The sweep of history favors progressive ideals and social justice—that is a truism proven every day. As the country embraced gay marriage, gun control, legalized marijuana, and said "NO!" to a war in Syria, and doesn't seem very hot on reigniting the cold war, politicians and news anchors had to play catch up with the American people.

HOW TO USE THIS BOOK

Over the years, I've been observing the American political scene as it portrays itself through the media. I've collected the little moments in the discourse where the cracks are showing. Through these cracks escapes some failed deception or truth, enabling me to make my own cracks. These fragments form a twitching mosaic that tell the bigger story of what's wrong in America.

It's all here, from the inconsequential to the important stuff. And don't let the occasional numbers and facts fool you: beneath this book's snarky juvenile exterior hides a deeply immature inner soul that is also pissed off.

Flip through the book the same as you would switch channels with your remote control. If you think a section stinks, I promise it'll be over soon (I wish I could say the same about Joyce Carol Oates novels). I hit upon different aspects of the same problem only because I think certain points are worth hammering into the ground.

If the jokes seem to hit below the beltway, it is only because I don't take these people as seriously as they take themselves.

Don't feel sorry for anyone skewered in this book. From years of observation I can tell you that they lack shame, they don't feel pain, and they don't feel pain for others (unless there's a camera on). The fact that they're laughing all the way to the bank means that we should laugh harder behind their backs.

If you purchase this book for no other reason than as something you can throw at these people, I'll be happy.

INTRODUCTION: NOT POLITICAL

"Do you pay attention to your fucking life?!"

In retrospect, it wasn't the most tactful thing I could have said.

I was talking to Greg, a friend from my old neighborhood, whom I hadn't seen in years. I was born on the South Side of Chicago in a family of 12 kids. They say you learn a lot about life growing up in a big family. The biggest thing I learned was that I was easily replaced.

I knew that, if I died, it wasn't going to put a big dent in my parents' plans. Can't imagine my mom sitting around crying, "Oh no, Jimmy's gone! What am I going to do now . . . with just the ELEVEN OF YOU? How do I fill the empty 1/12th of my heart?"

I grew up in a blue-collar neighborhood. It was *really* blue collar . . . you know, racist.

The part of town I grew up voted for the Democrats for the better part of a century, until the first African-American Democratic candidate for mayor appeared on the ticket. Suddenly, my part of town realized they were actually Republicans.

These were the people who worked all day in physically demanding jobs they hated. After work, they'd stop at the bar to down a six pack while complaining about minorities and then go home to watch reruns of Archie Bunker . . . and laugh for all the wrong reasons. They didn't understand that they were supposed to be laughing at Archie Bunker, not with him. I used to run through my house yelling, "No, Meathead is right! Meathead is right!"

They loved to brag about how physically hard their jobs were. It was a weird macho competition where the winner was the guy who had the shittiest job.

"I worked a double shift on a stand-up forklift in a warehouse without air conditioning, in temperatures over 120 degrees," or "I started plowing snow at midnight on Friday, didn't stop until Sunday at 6pm. That's right, 40 hours straight at TRIPLE TIME!" was the kind of bragging you'd hear from guys in my neighborhood.

The only thing better than working a job that would put you into an early grave was having a job that paid well and required no work. Think toll booth operator. I know it sounds like a job you would try to avoid, but in my neighborhood, guys vigorously pursued these jobs. Toll booth workers were admired cuz they got to sit on their ass all day and got Dental.

A job at a major utility was also great for not working. My friend Danny worked for the Commonwealth Edison, the company that powered Chicago, and his favorite brag was "Today I spent 8 hours looking for a pipe. . . . Guess what? I didn't find it!" And he would laugh as if he had beaten life.

Of course the only job that could top them all was Chicago city fireman—the crown jewel of blue-collar jobs. Respect and envy ran deep for the fireman, for they could trump any occupational brag. A fireman could both boast about not working at all and having to do the hardest, most dangerous work in the world.

Chicago city firemen had 24-hour shifts, and consequently, they only went into work 7 days a month. Basically they spent their shifts sleeping, eating, or playing cards. So most of their time they were getting paid union wages to do nothing. But at the bar, they could also tell stories about climbing three flights of stairs in pitch-black smoke and carrying down a 300-pound elderly lady. Not that these firemen were slackers. Most worked heavy-duty second jobs in their off-hours, like carpentry or bricklaying, driving their co-workers nuts by boasting about getting paid for sleeping at the firehouse.

Those were the exceptions. This was a world where hard work wasn't shunned but embraced. These men worked until their bodies burned out. They sacrificed for their families and for the American promise that, if you worked hard, you could have a good middle-class life. Sadly, that is no longer the case. This is a different America.

We are now a nation in which workers live near the poverty line, where social mobility is stuck in quicksand, wages barely support a family, and third world labor forces making first-world products is the norm. We innovate financial schemes like derivatives, credit default swaps, and mortgage backed securities—all things that create money for the money changers and add nothing to the economy or society. Which leads me back to my friend Greg.

My friend Greg was now living in St. Louis. In the fall of 2008 I visited him. He used to be a mortgage broker. I say "used to," because he lost his job when, um, well . . . you know (like I said, it was 2008).

Greg was going through all the new American rites of passage: out of work, lost his health insurance, upside-down on his own house. All of this while raising a family with one kid in college, the other in Afghanistan, and a wife with a medical condition. He was in a tough spot, and I couldn't have felt more sorry for him. And worst of all, he lives in St. Louis.

He told me that nobody saw the financial crisis coming. Nobody? All the brainiacs in the banking business, the guys on Wall Street buying and selling mortgage securities, the federal regulators—none of them had a clue that a train wreck of 1930s proportions was on its way? There were some pretty big train wrecks in the 1930s . . . oh, and there was also the Great Depression.

I'm a comedian. If comedy were about to make millions of people lose their homes and cause giant, 100-year-old banks to fail, I think I would try to warn people. Hell, I tried to warn people about Dane Cook and Jay Leno. If I didn't see something like that coming, expert that I am supposed to be, I would at least feel like a dick for a super long time.

However, I was conflicted. Greg has always stayed gleefully igno-rant of politics and current events that are not celebrity- or sports-related. So I thought it was kind of sad that it took this horrible turn of events and the shittiest government since the invention of shitty governments to make my friend politically aware. At the same time, I was a little happy. I thought that, from then on, we would engage each other in conversations of substance and import. Our time together would be meaningful, and maybe we would even grow closer (not that I really care, I have enough friends, I tell myself).

I was eager to begin, and blurted out my conversation-starter: "So, who are you voting for?"

"Oh, I don't pay attention to politics," Greg said matter-of-factly.

"Well, do you pay attention to your fucking LIFE!?" I replied, with my conversation-ender. Maybe I could have been more tactful and gone with, "OK, if you could have lunch with any politician, living or dead, who would it be? And would you ask them about the deregulated financial system that put you in the poor house?"

That evening I returned to my hotel, counting how many friends I had left, and on television I heard this:

"As you know, I'm not political at all on my show."
–Andy Cohen, television host

That was said by openly gay television host Andy Cohen. He was making the rounds on TV talking about gay rights and how important they are . . . but please don't forget that he's not political at all, except, I guess, when he stops to talk about the most incendiary political topic of our time. Then he's political.

Yeah, it'd be nice if every "non-political" person's pet issue wasn't inextricably connected to every other political issue in the whole world. Saying you're "not political" and then talking about gay marriage and civil rights is like calling yourself a vegetarian when you eat chickens and pandas. Andy Cohen is an openly gay TV host, for

Christ's sake! That in itself is a *huge* political statement.

We are all political. If you want the pothole in front of your house fixed, that's politics. If you want better schools for your kids, that's politics. If you don't want your tax dollars wasted on foreign wars, that's politics. If you want clean air and water, that's politics. If you want to be able to go to the doctor when you get sick without going bankrupt, that's politics. And if you want equality for gay people under the law, that is not only political, but to a lot of people, including lots of good white Christians, that's also radical.

Most things are considered radical until they aren't anymore, like slavery. That was pretty radical. Oh yeah, owning and enslaving other people was a real hot-button political issue; it was the "gay rights" of its day. Imagine Abraham Lincoln saying, "I'm calling for completely changing the economic model for half the country to assure equal rights for all people . . . but don't worry, this isn't political."

Why does this bother me? Is it because the Andy Cohens of the world think it makes them more mature to say, "I'm not political!"? I guess it bothers me because I know people like that. The people who like to play the nice, happy-go-lucky guy that everybody likes, who isn't strident like those "political types." Get it? He'll never do anything that is the least off-putting, and he certainly won't say anything to make you question your beliefs.

It creates this false world of "getting along just fine without politics." As if nice people, friendly people, likable people don't talk about politics. My friend Greg said folks in St. Louis "don't like to have those kinds of conversations."

Even when their lives are crushed by a collapsed unregulated economy, they act as if politics is a luxury, reserved for people with too much time on their hands. As if government has as much relevance to their lives as Arena Football. I just don't get that mentality. They could be a Jew in 1932 Germany and be voting for Hitler. "I don't pay attention to politics, I let the guy with the little mustache take care of stuff. I've got other stuff to do, you know?"

Not that the media makes it easy for them to get informed. Who would've guessed that corporate made-for-profit news might be less than informative? Some media outlets are actual defense contractors, like NBC and MSNBC, which are 49% owned by General Electric, which sucks more than $1.8 billion out of the Pentagon's tit every year. Trying to get the truth about a war from these multinational corporations is like trying to get the truth from someone . . . who is not inclined to give it to you! . . . (OK, my analogies are wanting, and I didn't want to mention Hitler and the Jews again, but I'm taking a class at the Learning Annex.)

In fact, most people are so misinformed that they still believe the myth that news is controlled by a "Liberal Media." My friend recently said he doesn't watch NBC, "because they're too liberal." Hmmm . . . a liberal defense contractor full of vegetarian hippies manufacturing hemp-knitted cruise missiles, makes sense.

Me? I sometimes wish I were the kind of person who only watched Fox News. I like my news given to me straight, exactly how the Koch brothers, the Heritage Foundation, and Rupert Murdoch want me to hear it. Don't waste your audience's time by getting all fact-checky about the supposed information you're broadcasting. What good does that do? I mean, let's say you discover that politicians are stating incorrect "facts" (which they usually are). What then? They're just going to keep doing exactly whatever they want, whether it's bad for the country or just super-bad (and I don't mean black-exploitation-movie kind of "super-bad," I mean the way the words were actually meant to mean). So now all you've done is upset yourself because you know the "truth." I've seen it happen to people I love. My brother only watches Bill Moyers on PBS, and now he walks around anxious and miserable all the time. Bill Moyers and his crew are always investigating and finding out stuff, like facts.

They're constantly exposing the current administration's lies, propaganda, and spin. Yet it hasn't changed a thing, and my brother has
developed a bleeding ulcer.

It's enough to make you move to St. Louis.

WHAT'S
WRONG
WITH
THE MEDIA?

"I don't think we [shape perceptions of the Iraq war] . . . but we try."
–Rupert Murdoch, Australian

The Media is owned by five guys. I know this because I had it explained to me when I was on mushrooms, and I had clarity.

Rupert Murdoch is the boss of those guys. He owns everything. I'm kidding . . . a little. He only controls all the news and information in most of the world. Stuff like the *Wall Street Journal*, NewsCorp, Twentieth Century Fox, Direct TV, Sky TV, Fox News, the *New York Post*, the *Chicago Sun-Times*, the *Village Voice* (how did that happen?), the *Boston Herald*, London's *Sunday Times*, and most TV in Europe, Asia, and Australia . . . OK, you get the point, right? Because if not, I could list *TV Guide*, the *Sun*, five more British national newspapers, most of England's satellite TV, and oh yeah, he also bought MySpace.

And then he bought the Dow Jones.

Did you read that last part? He bought the Dow Jones. Which (I have to be honest here) I didn't know you could fucking do! Seriously, you can buy the STOCK MARKET??!! How much money does that guy have?!

I would love to be a fly on the wall in his office. I imagine him sitting in his whale-skin chair, stroking a Persian cat with a diamond collar . . .

Murdoch: I think I want to buy a business.

Lackey: All right sir, which business would you like to purchase?

Murdoch: Hmm . . . ALL of THEM.

Lackey: Wow, ballsy move sir. Well played. Anything else you would like to acquire while I'm at it?

Murdoch: Yes . . . THE ALPHABET!

Lackey: Well, that one is going to cost you.

Murdoch: Well skip "Q," I don't need "Q"; it will be quicker that way . . . Wait! I do need "Q"!!

Then, I imagine he presses a button that burns a barrel of oil just for kicks.

You may be asking, "But Jimmy, how does this affect me? What do I care who owns a satellite company, or a newspaper which I don't read?"

If you get all your information from the Media, and the Media is owned by a handful of dudes who want to go to war, what do you think they'd do?

First thing, scare the shit out of everyone! Do I even need to point this out? Watch any television newscast, and I dare you not to shit your pants, metaphorically and literally. Double dare! Sissy.

If you listen to the Media, Al Qaeda members are ten feet tall and made out of titanium. They're also a special kind of crazy. A crazy we've never seen before! Look out! These Al Qaeda are crazier than Charlie Manson!!

In reality, Al Qaeda is just a bunch of cavemen that had one good day . . . and they had to buy a plane ticket to do it. Seriously, they don't even own a plane, for fuck's sake.

"I'm going to blow you up in the name of ALLAH! . . . But I got bumped, and I'm on standby . . . this is so embarrassing." Makes you almost feel sorry for the little terrorist without Orbitz.

No matter what, though, the Media needs us to feel afraid of the TERROR! They have kept us scared. How scared? Well, think about this: We were so scared in America after 9/11 that you couldn't make fun of the president anymore. At least I couldn't, and I used to make fun of Ronald Reagan! And people loved Ronald Reagan! Fuckin' loved him! Because people love the guy that looks like what a president is supposed to look like, even if he is raping them . . . right in the asshole . . . that they shit out of. People loved him so much they buried him three times (and at none of his funerals did anybody remember to drive a stake through his heart).

So after 9/11, we found ourselves here, in the United States of America, where we treasure our right to lampoon our elected officials. We hold it as sacrosanct as a congressman's third marriage. We had the biggest moron in the White House since people started saying "moron." People were so scared they would yell at you for making a joke about the president.

Case in point: Shortly after 9/11, I was doing some George W. Bush jokes at a club in Houston (because I'm brilliant!), and I got the strangest heckle I ever gotten in my career. Out of the darkness, I heard, "Hey, he's protecting your freedom of speech! Now shut the fuck up!"

Wow, it was weird. For the first time in my life, I was caught in a riddle.

Just a few weeks later, I was in Ft. Lauderdale (again, I am brilliant!). Right in the middle of the same Bush jokes, a guy flips me off with *both hands* (which I guess he did so I would not mistake this for a casual or pleasant flip-off), and yells, "Fuck you! Go back to your Jew state!"

"Um, dude," I said, "We're in Florida. You might want to icksnay on the ew-Jay. They're all around us."

The point is, we are sufficiently scared. Now we can be manipulated. Let's say your government wants to start an illegal war. Maybe invade a country that isn't a threat, but has shit-loads of oil (and I'm talking metric shit-loads here). However, they can't just say that is what they are going to do. So, they concoct a story, but they need someone to sell it to you. Bingo! How about the guy who owns most of the media in Australia, Britain, and the U.S.? And those are the three main countries going along with Bush's brilliant war! And the guy with all the media really wants this war, too! It's almost like God wanted it this way!

I'm sure it's all just a coincidence.

So, there you are: scared, with no home, no healthcare, and $5 per gallon gas, and your government has no funds to help you, because it's all sitting in a hole called Iraq.

That's how it affects you. Suck it.

BRIAN WILLIAMS, CITIZEN

"I try to play it down the middle, like you do every night. I do it in news; you do it in comedy. We try not to take a side."
–*NBC Nightly News* anchor Brian Williams, speaking with Jimmy Fallon

I would suggest that Brian Williams is bold-faced lying in his assertion that he plays it right down the middle. Am I suggesting he has a liberal or conservative bias? No, I'm saying he doesn't play it down the middle, because he doesn't play it at all.

Being a stenographer for anybody who can issue a press release or stage a press event is not playing. And by playing, I mean being an actual journalist. Why does the number one newsman in America give credence to the theory that there are two sides to the news? I didn't know that there were two sides to the truth. Good thing he is not trying to do this "down the middle" corporate tool reporting in

England. How do you play it down the middle in a country with *three* major political parties?

"Play it right down the middle"? I don't even know what the hell sport he's referring to where a third party throws a ball between two other competing parties. That analogy is shitty. Would it have been so hard for him to say, "Look, I just show up and read out loud whatever is put in front of me and look good doing it. I honestly don't know or think hardly anything except that I sure like being famous and stuff." The reporter for the *PennySaver* asks more questions than *NBC Nightly News* does.

> **"At the end of the day when I clock out, I'm a citizen.**
> **I vote—I don't discuss how I vote—I pay taxes, I have**
> **opinions, and I don't like this brinkmanship about the**
> **debt limit of the United States. Real Americans are going**
> **to get real hurt if they don't raise this."**
> **–Brian Williams on *Late Night with Jimmy Fallon***

Oh, so after a long day, Brian takes off his journalist coat, and he's just an everyday guy who pays taxes and votes—and that's when he has his private opinions. Does that make sense to anyone else? "Hey, I go to a job where I am given huge amounts of information, but I do not form any critical position regarding that information. But, you know, at the end of the day, I go home, and have all my opinions, but without the information I got at work."

What the fuck?

Notice how our hero pretends that it is both parties being reckless and unreasonable and then leaves out the pertinent information about a small group of extreme right-wing ideologues being reckless enough to ruin our economy.

Sooooooo, according to Brian Williams, reporting who is responsible for the debt ceiling debate is partisan journalism. But! Not reporting who is responsible for the ongoing debt ceiling debacle is "playing it down the middle."

Then Brian says, as a private citizen with opinions, he doesn't like this "brinkmanship," which is taking the debt ceiling debate right to the last minute. Wait, as a private citizen with opinions, Brian, who do you blame for this? Or am I speaking to Newsman Brian? OK, Newsman Brian, what are the predominate political forces that have caused this crisis, which has not happened since 1917? Oh, turns out neither Brian Williams is useful.

> **". . . [if the debt limit isn't raised] federal employees could stop getting paid, a lot of construction projects would halt, our credit rating would receive real damage, people's interest rates would go up . . . alternate side of the street parking will be suspended (laughter)."**

But, at the last minute, one of the Brian Williams personas (you can't tell which: "Is it my sister or my daughter? My sister or my daughter? It's Chinatown, Brian!") actually delivers some interesting information: the objectively understood consequences of a national default—and then, just before he says something really great, he ends it with a softball joke about parking in New York City. It was creepy. Like he lost control of his passions and actually started to give us an informed perspective, but then realized he had gone too far and covered it with a joke so Jimmy Fallon will continue to like him.

Mr. Williams, I know it makes you cringe to actually report facts that will upset your corporate masters or half the dimwits in your audience . . . but that's your job, Brian. It is your job TO SIFT THROUGH THE BULLSHIT and tell the people what it MEANS.

Now, I full on expect that one day I'll be watching the NBC Nightly News, and Brian Williams will give us an actual thorough piece of news with an objective critical analysis, and then will suddenly say, "Oh no, I've said too much." Then a shot will ring out, and just as Brian is sinking below the desk, the broadcast will switch to an emergency lost episode of *Will & Grace* that NBC keeps on standby, just in case.

I used to think Brian Williams was the problem—now I realize Brian Williams was the only guy from central casting they could get who wouldn't stop mid-broadcast and say, "Are you fucking kidding me! There's some serious shit going on out there, and this is what we're talking about?!"

HERE TODAY, JUAN TOMORROW

**"Has it ever occurred to you that conservatives *are*
the media?"**
—Juan Williams, house liberal, Fox News

That was Juan Williams schooling Amy Holmes after she denied that Republicans have a more reliable media base to disseminate their message than the Democrats.

Not that she'll drop the old "the media is liberal" canard, because that's what it said in her morning spam email of conservative talking points.

The whole thing started when Howard Kurtz quoted Bill Clinton:

Kurtz: "Bill Clinton told CNN that Republicans have a much more reliable media base than Democrats, is that true?"

Holmes: "Conservatives are piled on continuously by the media; we see that the media loves nothing more than when Republicans are turning on one another."

Williams: "Has it ever occurred to you that conservatives are the media? Don't you work for The Blaze?"

Holmes: "I do work for The Blaze."

Williams: "Don't you know about the Drudge Report, and Red State and Fox News?"

Holmes: "Are you saying we have the same amount of power as the *New York Times* and the *Washington Post*?"

Williams: "The *Wall Street Journal* is the number one newspaper and the most conservative editorial page in the nation."

Holmes: "But not conservative on the reporting side."

Williams: "Thank God."

What . . . what the hell is this? Who . . . ?

So, there's Howard Kurtz, Fox News' media critic, which is a joke almost on an existential level, even funnier than a guy getting fired from a show named *Reliable Sources* for filing too many stories that were unreliable.

He's got this panel in front of him . . . which . . . is everything a fucking panel now? I get that it stirs up conversation, but it also seems extraordinarily lazy at times; like it's a way for everyone, the moderator in particular, to avoid responsibility for what's being said. Also, how often do I want to watch my news in the same format as my terrible family Thanksgivings? I seriously wouldn't be surprised at all if, for example, Rahm Emanuel was on *Meet the Press* and drunkenly stood up and declared he could "say the n-word in his own goddamn house if he wanted to!" This also might be better journalism than its current format.

"You work for The Blaze, don't you?"

"I do work for The Blaze."

Then what the fuck are you doing on the panel? Or anywhere else for that matter? For those who don't know, The Blaze is a sort of TV station/website started by Glenn Beck. Glenn Beck was released from Fox News because . . . **he was too conservative and insane for Fox News!** It's a basketful of conspiracy theories and insane libertarian talking points. Saying you work for The Blaze is like saying you work for a militia newsletter.

"The *Wall Street Journal* is the number one newspaper, and the most conservative editorial page in the nation."

"But . . . not on the reporting side."

There it is! Lady, that's called journalism. You know, a series of facts reported in context so as to create an accurate picture of an event or other phenomena? By its definition it is not partisan. Except that it is, because accurate reporting runs counter to the conservative narrative in which Reagan never raised taxes and teenagers won't get pregnant if you never tell them about sex.

And this really is the heart of the matter. The Right has been claiming, since forever, that the media is overwhelmingly liberal. This is what they mean: They mean actual information is inherently liberal.

One of two things is going on here: This lady either genuinely believes what she's saying, or she really doesn't. If she does, then wow, she's super stupid—or maybe grew up in some kind of Koch brothers re-education camp. If she doesn't believe what she's saying, well then, she's playing an old and ugly game, like Parcheesi with your dick out.

Claiming the media is liberal serves the Right in two ways:

• First, it paints the Right as victims. Which . . . yuck. The sight of white, rich men preserving the dominant paradigm claiming they are victims is really gross.

• Second, it casts doubt on pretty much all reporting that goes against the conservative agenda. So, if the Washington Post publishes a series of articles that expose, let's say, a presidential conspiracy to commit felonies, well, it can be dismissed by the party faithful as a typical liberal hatchet job.

Oh, and by the way, this lady isn't even responding to what Kurtz is suggesting. Kurtz isn't talking about the news. He's talking about the "Republican Media Base," meaning its messaging system—which is *much more reliable* than the Democrats'. How do I know this? Well, the Democrats somehow failed to communicate a case for single-payer healthcare, and the Republicans managed to get everyone to believe there would be death panels.

So, yes, the Republican media base is more reliable. The main-stream media, and even truly liberal media, are independent actors, whereas the right-wing media outlets seem to act in lock-step with one another. Seriously, next time there is some major partisan issue in the news, take a look around. What you will find is Fox News, The Daily Caller, and the Drudge Report all reporting the same talking points, pretty much word for word. It's both comforting in its consistency and terrifying in its malevolence—like German fairy tales or *Project Runway*.

BROKAW'S BROKEN JOURNALISM

"Congressman Ryan <u>overreached</u> a few times and got caught in those <u>overreaches</u>, so that's a problem for the Republicans in <u>overreaching</u> . . . when they overreach, it goes to their credibility . . . the American people are out there saying 'we don't know who to believe.'"
–Tom Brokaw, corporate news obfuscator

Yeah, Paul Ryan "overreached" . . . to help you understand the word, some other famous "overreachers" are Bernie Madoff, Lance Armstrong, Dick Cheney, and O.J. Simpson.

That was Tom Brokaw's assessment of vice presidential nominee Paul Ryan's speech that was so jaw-droppingly dishonest and full of lies that even Fox News debunked him and called him a liar.

> "Ryan's speech was an apparent attempt to set the world record for the greatest number of blatant lies and misrepresentations slipped into a single political speech."
> –FoxNews.com

So why wouldn't Tom Brokaw call out Ryan's lies? Mostly out of habit, but also because Brokaw is afraid if he says, "Paul Ryan is lying," he'll be considered liberally biased—and that is like kryptonite to a mainstream newsperson. So instead of running the risk of a conservative hack accusing him of liberal bias, Tom Brokaw shows that he'd much rather be full of shit.

Network journalists can't call politicians "liars" because that's crossing the line into a no-man's land where you're telling the truth, exposing corruption, and changing things for the better.

Why would a reporter call a lying politician a liar? All that would do is accurately describe the situation and give your viewers a clearer picture of what is actually happening. I appreciate a newsman who relies on his viewers' ability to read between the lines.

Better to soft-pedal and sugarcoat the truth, because that's what the American people are constantly asking for: "Please Mr. TV Newsman, don't give it to us straight, please try to make it harder to understand what is really going on."

Overreach? It would be an overreach to call Tom Brokaw a journalist.

MESSAGE ON JIMMY'S VOICEMAIL:

BILL O'REILLY, 12:23 PM

Jimmy Dore, this is Bill O'Reilly.

You liberal arugula munchers should be happy with my latest social campaign. As you know, the Factor helps minority children at risk all across the country. They make up most of my audience.

So, I'm going after the biggest problem facing the black community: Sexy music videos.

Yes, you heard me. Music videos are causing the devastation of unwanted pregnancies and fractured families in black neighborhoods.

Did you see the latest video by Beyoncé? I didn't like it.

All these teenage black girls who watch VH-1 are being corrupted by the likes of Beyoncé and Alicia Keys. It's got to stop Jimmy, simple as that.

That Rahm Emmanuel has the right idea. He's shut down 47 neighborhood public schools in Chicago. The only way to help poor families is to force their little brats into private schools. Education problem solved. Finally there's a Democrat with some common sense.

You should take a page out his book, Jimbo. Speaking of book, I hear that you have a book coming out. If I find out there's anything about me in it, my next book will be "Killing Jimmy Dore".

Do you know who the real victim of racism is? The Racists. That's right. These are people who are persecuted for their beliefs.

Think about the discrimination they have to face, day-in day-out. They're becoming the real minority in this country. I don't see you liberal pinheads fighting against the bigotry shown to them in our culture.

Talking point memo: Obamacare is a colossal failure. The cheaper premiums are killing Americans. I want my pre-existing conditions back.

One hour 'til I do my show. I have to go paint my bald spot.

HEY, ASSHOLE!–CHRIS MATTHEWS

"I'm so glad we had [Hurricane Sandy] last week . . . the storm brought in possibilities for good politics."
–Chris Matthews,
    fluorescent-haired douchebag

That's a great point, and I'm glad Chris Matthews had the guts to make it. Let's face it, a catastrophic disaster that destroyed people's lives is a small price to pay for Obama getting a boost in his favorability rating, am I right?

Besides, way too many people in New Jersey were living comfortably in their homes with all their possessions intact anyway. To be fair, Chris Matthews did try to backtrack and say that when he "thanked God" for Hurricane Sandy that he meant it politically, not in terms of hurting people.

I hear you Chris, I think politically too, and I was thinking about those 100 people who died in Hurricane Sandy, and I thought, "Thank God it didn't affect the popular vote!" And then I thought, "I bet Chris Matthews would be proud of me right now."

Now that he's offended a few million flood victims in New York and New Jersey, tune in tomorrow night for his ham-fisted apology.

But let's remember—Chris Matthews still hasn't apologized for all the great things he said about President Bush right after 9/11.

CONVERSATION WITH THE WORLD'S LUCKIEST INTERN

JIMMY DORE: Luke, you caused a bit of a stir when you asked Nancy Pelosi if she might be too old for her job.

LUKE RUSSERT: What's the big deal, Jimmy? All I did was raise a legitimate issue.

JIMMY DORE: Which is?

LUKE RUSSERT: That old people suck. Come on Jimmy, it's true. Have you ever been in a car on the freeway stuck behind an intelligent woman who's worked for decades to become a highly qualified professional? It friggin' blows, man!

JIMMY DORE: Luke, some are saying that you're the last person who should be questioning someone on their qualifications for a job.

LUKE RUSSERT: Whoa, Jimmy, are you actually bringing up the tragic death of my father, Tim Russert?

JIMMY DORE: Yes, I am.

LUKE RUSSERT: Well, I wish you wouldn't, because I don't feel comfortable talking about the biggest break of my career.

When something that awesome happens, it's best to keep it to yourself.

JIMMY DORE: But everybody already knows that you only got your job because of nepotism.

LUKE RUSSERT: That is so unfair, dude! I am totally qualified for my job.

JIMMY DORE: How so?

LUKE RUSSERT: Well, Tim Russert was my father, and I was his son. Therefore I was more than qualified for a nepotistic gig when it became available.

JIMMY DORE: But then don't you understand that people take umbrage when you say that Nancy Pelosi and the Democratic leadership should step aside for others just because those others are younger?

LUKE RUSSERT: Okay, but by the same token, people who get jobs totally based on merit are standing in the way of someone who wants that job solely based on the biological accident of their birth. It works both ways, Jimmy. Both sides do it! Both sides do it!

JIMMY DORE: You're not making any sense.

LUKE RUSSERT: Jimmy, did you ever read my dad's book about my granddad, *Big Russ And Me*? I told my father he should call that book, Why Don't You Just Die, You Old Fuck. I mean, Dad used to always make me visit Big Russ's house, it smelled like peanut brittle covered in poop. Big Russ would kiss me on my cheek, and I'd have a gummy, slurping oldnguy hickey on my face for weeks. I'm a reporter, Jimmy. I'm supposed to report the truth. And the truth is that elderly old coots are grody to the max.

JIMMY DORE: Well, Luke Russert, thanks for joining us today.

LUKE RUSSERT: Jimmy, I just want to remind you of one thing.

JIMMY DORE: What's that?

LUKE RUSSERT: I'll have made more money by the time I'm thirty than you will make in your entire pathetic life.

JIMMY DORE: That's probably true. Thanks for sharing.

PRESS THE MEAT

"In too many parts of the world, America is no longer seen as a reliable ally or an enemy to be feared, nor do our adversaries any longer fear us."
–David Gregory quoting Liz Cheney on *Meet the Press*, 2012

Oh thank God, someone from the Bush administration—the masters of foreign policy in the Middle East—is here to tell all of us which way the wind is blowing. And that's weird too, because that very same week, the Bush twins told a reporter from *Tiger Beat* that Iran is stupid.

How does a woman, whose only claim to fame is being the daughter of a war criminal, continue to get booked on national news shows and get quoted on them when she isn't? Because the news media sucks and will bring on anyone who repeats corporate talking points.

So, this is part of a concerted effort to undermine the president's perceived strength in foreign policy—and instead of debunking it and calling it out, David Gregory *repeats* it. (And just letting you know, under a Liz Cheney administration, Egyptian and Libyan rioters would be terrified of us, and we would be on the brink of war with Iran pretty much every second.)

Liz Cheney: Hey, Dad?

Darth Cheney: Yes, Liz?

Liz Cheney: Why don't people fear and respect the United States anymore?

Darth Cheney: Well, we elected a black guy.

Liz Cheney: But besides that.

Darth Cheney: Well, it might have something to do with the fact that your Uncle George and I spent two or three trillion dollars waging war in the Middle East, thereby making it almost impossible for the U.S. to find the political and actual capital necessary to really threaten Iran. Oh, and we took out the regime of Saddam Hussein, which was one of the few direct checks Iran had in the region.

Liz Cheney: Should I say that in my op-ed to the *Wall Street Journal*?

Darth Cheney: I'd rather you didn't.

SHITTY MEDIA–JIM CRAMER STYLE

Of all the pretend financial reporters that missed the housing bubble and failed to predict the collapse of the economy brought on by Wall Street, Jim Cramer is certainly the loudest. He proves you don't even have to know what you're talking about, as long as you're constantly shouting. Cramer also has the uncanny ability to predict major recessions years after they've hit. I've watched *Mad Money* many times, and I wouldn't ask Jim Cramer's advice on how to get to the freeway.

"Health insurance is an expense that could save your life . . . medical expenses are the number one cause of bankruptcy, so don't get wiped out . . . save room in your budget for health insurance!!"
–Jim Cramer, CNBC ass-clown

Cramer also advises that people get jobs to keep from going broke and to eat food to keep from starving to death.

Next, Cramer shows us how you can be an idiot and still make millions of dollars by hosting a show on CNBC.

PHONE CALL FROM TOM BROKAW

JIMMY: Tom, I've noticed the odd way you're reporting about the Tea Party. You make no mention of the fact that the Tea Party is funded by corporate interests who are duping low information voters.

TOM: Look Jimmy, the Tea Party is what I like to call a grass-roots organization.

JIMMY: But most of their money comes from the Koch brothers.

TOM: And the Koch brothers get most of their money from coal and oil, don't they?

JIMMY: So how is that grassroots?

TOM: Coal makes electricity and oil makes gas, and who uses more electricity and gas than Americans? So the money is really coming from average Americans.

JIMMY: That is about the biggest bunch of bullshit I've ever heard.

TOM: Well Jimmy, it may turn out to be bullshit or it may not, but I've found that if you say something with a pensive look on your face, it makes people think you're smart.

JIMMY: But you are smart . . . aren't you, Tom?

TOM: Well, Jimmy . . .

JIMMY: Come on Tom, you may live in your completely out-of-touch bubble surrounded by millionaires and sycophants, but you're not dumb.

TOM: Dumb enough to go into broadcasting with a speech impediment. But smart enough to deliver the news in a way that avoids stepping on rich and powerful toes, while climbing the corporate ladder like a spider monkey.

JIMMY: So you are actually not smart.

TOM: Did you see the movie *Broadcast News*? Do you remember William Hurt's character? How he came across as informed, concerned, and dignified, while he was really a vacant, shallow corporate climber who looked at the news not as an important safeguard of democracy, but as an acting exercise?

JIMMY: You're not telling me it is actually that bad.

TOM: No, I'm telling you it's worse. I make *Broadcast News* look like Edward R. Murrow. I got an award from the military; that's how I know I'm doing my job right.

JIMMY: That's disappointing.

TOM: You know what is really disappointing, the eggs on my muffin. I like them runny, and they're overdone. Listen Jim, I gotta go, working on new book.

JIMMY: What's it about?

TOM: Well, I like to stay one step ahead of my colleagues, and I know that the white population continues to shrink here in America. Instead of pandering to old whitey, I'm writing a book that preemptively sucks up to the new brown majority, The Greatest Immigration. All about how immigrants make our lives better by nannying our kids and cleaning our cars.

NEWS FLASHED—PROFILES IN COURAGE

In the summer of 2013, Amazon founder and CEO Jeff Bezos bought the *Washington Post*. Bezos acquired the newspaper for 250 million dollars in cash, 10 million of which he'd been keeping in the front seat of his car to pay tolls. Insiders say Bezos could've gotten the paper for a few million less, but he really wanted the two-day shipping.

Over the past couple of years, the *Post* has lost 75 million dollars . . . but Bezos believes that with a meticulous business plan going forward, he could easily blow twice that. Selling the paper was a painful decision for the Graham family, or as painful as any decision that gets you 250 million dollars in cash.

Bezos is excited about the challenge of making the legendary paper available to a whole new generation that won't read it. The Amazon tycoon says he's proud of helping to keep a great newspaper in business, though his work won't really be complete until every store in America has closed.

Amazon currently employs 100,000 warehouse workers throughout the world, 73 of whom are happy. The pay is low, and the conditions are oppressive. But on the bright side, eventually you get fired for not working fast enough. It's been said Amazon workers have even been let go for bursting into tears on the job . . . which explains why, when those *Washington Post* employees heard who bought their newspaper, they kept on smiling.

Their new boss reassured them that nothing would change, except their fate was now in the hands of a self-made billionaire who does whatever he wants.

TIRED OF FATIGUE

"Americans are suffering from Apocalypse fatigue. They have been told for the last forty years that they're going to die from 'nuclear winter,' 'global cooling,' global warming, and they hear now that [the debt ceiling] is Armageddon. I don't think they believe it."
–George F. Will, columnist with hair combed like a toupee

I have always assumed that sometime in the 1960s, a hippie stole George Will's girlfriend. He then vowed to become a columnist and pundit and really stick it to those hippie liberal communists with their smoldering good looks and sexually exciting political views. Well, true to his vow, George never misses an opportunity to belittle those No Nukes flower children and those crunchy homosexual environmentalists—even when he's being asked about a completely unrelated subject . . . like say, the debt ceiling.

Apocalypse fatigue? Yeah, it sure was crazy when people were concerned that two nations had hundreds of nuclear warheads pointed at one another—it's exactly the same as the guy standing on the corner screaming, "Get with Jesus, cuz The End is Near."

And oh man, those scientists with their insane predictions about climate change—that are demonstrably coming true—I mean, every time you talk to a climatologist, it's like they're saying the comet is coming and we need to take poison right now.

George Will, the elitist who speaks for the common man, theorizes that average Americans don't believe the dire predictions about the consequences of not raising the debt ceiling—predictions made by most economists, everyone on Wall Street, and the Treasury department—because they've heard too many fake apocalypse stories.

Isn't it more likely they don't believe it because they're dumb-asses?

You know, in a republic, it's not the average citizen's job to understand the complex issues of global economic policy. We are supposed to elect people who will understand these issues and act upon them with wisdom. It could be a good system, except when we start electing people who are "Just like us" and people who "We'd really like to have a beer with," because we'd be electing dumbasses like ourselves, and we sure as shit don't know what the hell is going on.

But of course, if George Will made that point, he wouldn't be able to put the screw to that long-haired draft dodger with his totally awesome van.

FALSE EQUIVALENCIES: THIS AND THAT

> **"The problem is the Democrats' focus was on this, the Republicans' focus was on that . . . and the focus is not on the common good but on individual party ideology . . ."**
> **–Mike Barnicle, explaining the failure of congressional budget negotiations**

He's right, the Democrats do focus on "*this*," but what exactly is "this"? Protecting Medicare and Social Security. Making sure the most vulnerable among us aren't now asked to carry the financial burden of fixing our economy when the people who have made a killing off this rigged economy get a tax cut.

And the Republicans focus on "*that*," meaning: Making sure to place the financial burden of fixing our economy on the backs of the people who can least afford it and who have been hurt the most by this rigged economy, the working poor and middle class.

See, they are both equally morally reprehensible. Right?

It's like during World War II, Nazis wanted to kill the Jews, while other people didn't, yet neither side would budge and come to a reasonable compromise—kill a few, save a few. These hardheads couldn't reach an agreement, and there was a war over it. (Don't know why I always reach for the Jews and Nazi Germany analogy all the time . . . I must be watching too much History Channel.)

Same thing in the 1860s: Lincoln was focused on emancipating the slaves, and the South wanted to keep them, and they were so dug in to their ideological positions that neither would budge. Like how 'bout they are slaves for half the day, and the other half, they are allowed to rest or find a second job to pay for stuff they want, like freedom?

This is what is wrong with America. The bastards that we have always fought got smart and bought the media, and they have effectively silenced true debate in our country in favor of agreed-upon corporate talking points.

And Mike Barnicle is a bag of liquid vagina cleaner, did I mention that? (That may sound like a juvenile outburst, but really it is a very sophisticated piece of satire.)

DEFACE THE NATION

They recently extended *Face the Nation* to a full hour (I know what you're thinking, but it only *felt* like an hour). Let's check to see how Bob Schieffer is using all that extra time.

> **"Today on *Face the Nation* . . . with the baseball post-season under way and Washington's team headed to the playoffs for the first time in 79 years, we'll talk baseball with the Dodgers' legendary manager Tommy Lasorda; Tony La Russa, manager of last year's World Champion St. Louis Cardinals; Jane Leavy, who wrote the book on**

Mickey Mantle and Peter Gammons of the MLB Network. It's Batter-Up on *Face the Nation*!"

Oh great, so Bob is using the extra half hour to do sports. Thank God *someone* is covering sports!!

My greatest hope is that Bob Schieffer asked his guests, "The Nationals and Baltimore are in the post-season—what does that mean to you?" And one of the guests said, "Nothing. It means absolutely nothing to me. It won't affect my tax burden or my healthcare or my retirement plans. What are you, stupid? Sports aren't important—they're supposed to be a distraction from what is important. Why is a supposed political program talking to Tommy fucking Lasorda?"

By the way, look at his "substantive" guest list:

David Axelrod–White House senior advisor

John Fund–*Wall Street Journal*

Michael Gerson–*Washington Post*

Norah O'Donnell–CBS

John Dickerson–CBS

Tommy Lasorda–MLB manager

Tony La Russa–MLB manager

Jane Leavy–sports writer

Peter Gammons–sports writer

Except for Axelrod, no one is actually in the practice of politics, and not one of them is in the middle of crafting real policy—you know, the laws that make a nation in order for us to face it.

None of those guests are rare visitors to television talking head land. Just try keeping any of those attention whores away from a camera; they'll bite your hand off. Lasorda alone will eat your arm to stay relevant.

I have faced the nation—and found it lacking.

FALSE EQUIVALENCIES:
THE GAY-MUSLIM ALLIANCE

"The homosexuals and Islamists work out of the same playbook."
—Tony Perkins, president of the Family Research Council

Who would have thought that the Tony Perkins who played Norman Bates would be the less psycho one? One of my pet peeves is the media's constant and insidious penchant for making false equivalencies about the Right and the Left, conservatives and progressives. Watching cable news, you'll notice the stomach-turning habit that many news hosts have of pretending that bigotry and ignorance is just a difference of opinion.

Tony Perkins is the president of the Family Research Council, an extreme Christian Coalition organization. They are anti-science and pro-ignorance, hiding behind religion in order to push hatred and bigotry.

Not the kind of guy you would call your friend, right? Here is supposed liberal Chris Matthews introducing Tony Perkins on his show:

"Tony, old pal! Thanks for joining us. I hope you don't get in trouble for me calling you 'old pal'!"

Instead of validating him, Matthews should be discrediting him . . . at least until the day when that gay suicide bomber fiercely explodes in a fabulous plume of glitter.

HEY ASSHOLE!–GEORGE STEPHANOPOULOS

"You said you love Kim [Jong-Un] and think he's awesome;
were you aware of his threat to destroy the United States
and his record on human rights? Do you think you have a
responsibility to ask him about it . . . "
  —George Stephanopoulos, speaking truth to
    ex-basketball players

That's George Snuffleupagus pretending to be a hard-hitting journalist
with somebody who can't hurt his social standing in Georgetown. I
find it ironic that a *Sunday morning news host* is criticizing someone
else for not asking the hard questions.

Really George, you're disappointed that Dennis Rodman didn't
ask harder questions? The hardest question I'd expect Dennis Rodman
to ask would be, "Is this North or South Korea?" This is why George is
still on top . . . he saves his tough questions for ex-basketball players.

George is in rare form and can't help himself:

Snuffles: "He puts 200,000 people in prison camps."

Rodman: "Well guess what? We do the same thing here."

Snuffles: "We have prison camps here in the USA?"

George is talking to a black man in America about *prison camps*
in *Korea*, and says we don't have prison camps in *America*.

America imprisons 2.4 million people. The United States has the
highest incarceration rate in the *world*. In fact, it's five to eight times
higher than the rest of the industrialized world. Since 1980, the
prison population has quadrupled, even though crime rates have
fallen dramatically in the last 25 years.

In 2008, 1 in every 31 adults was behind bars, on probation, or on parole. At year-end in 2007, the United States had less than 5% of the world's population but accounted for 23.4% of the world's prison and jail population.

Black males continue to be incarcerated at an extraordinary rate. Black males make up 35.4% of the jail and prison population—even though they make up less than 10% of the overall U.S population. 4% of U.S. black males were in jail or prison last year, compared to 1.7% of Hispanic males and .7% of white males. In other words, black males were locked up at almost six times the rate of their white counterparts.

So no George, we don't have prison camps in America; we have laws against calling them that. And do you know where I had to dig to find all that information about prisons, George? ABCnews.com.

One more asshole move by Snuffleup:

"Next time you go back (to North Korea), you should bring this report from Human Rights Watch; maybe ask him some questions about that."

Hey George, I know you like to hang with Donald Rumsfeld and his wife; how about *you* take the human rights report with you the next time you attend a party at a war criminal's house?

Next up, George discusses Iran's nuclear capability with Omarosa and Mike "the Situation."

"MISCHIEVOUS" MEDIA

"I have to admit, that I went on TV on Fox News and publicly engaged in what I guess was some rather mischievous speculation about whether Barack Obama really advocated socialism, a premise that privately I found rather far-fetched."
–Bill Sammon, Fox News executive

By 1983, the FCC had almost entirely abdicated any regulatory authority over cable television (so you could see boobs). In 1987, the Fairness Doctrine was removed from the FCC's general mandates. Fewer than ten years later, Fox News was launched on cable, which would not have been possible under the Fairness Doctrine and/or if the FCC had authority over cable TV.

In 1987, the most generous thinking on the matter went like this:

There are now enough media outlets that, in any given market, multiple political views on a given subject will be expressed. The press will now have even greater first amendment freedoms.

But that's not even close to what happened.

In 1987, news was not viewed as a money-making venture. Implicit in the Fairness Doctrine was the notion that media outlets had an obligation to expose and discuss issues that were important to the community.

By 1996, CNN had raked in untold profits for Turner Broadcasting, and there was more money on the table. Fox, unencumbered by the FCC, could get that money by playing to a specific audience: the audience that doesn't like to hear about global warming or evolution or gunshot victims. Fox News could get that audience and keep them by telling them exactly what they wanted to hear, 24 hours a day, seven days a week.

In 1987, a news show would have been terrified to report something inaccurate. They would have been horrified to present only one side of a political argument. They wouldn't present an editorial without a disclaimer. They would be in huge trouble if they tailored information to fit a specific agenda. If any of these things happened, they could easily lose their FCC license, and the whole station would go down the tubes. Now? Well, this is from an article in The Raw Story in 2011:

"Last year, candidate Barack Obama stood on a sidewalk in Toledo, Ohio and first let it slip to Joe the Plumber that he wanted to quote, 'spread the wealth around,'" Sammon said. "At that time, I have to admit, that I went on TV on Fox News and **publicly** engaged in what I guess was some rather mischievous speculation about whether Barack Obama really advocated socialism, a premise that privately I found rather far-fetched."

During the 2008 campaign, the then-Washington deputy managing editor repeatedly suggested that Obama had socialist tendencies.

On Oct. 14, 2008, Sammon said that Obama's comment to Joe Wurzelbacher "is red meat when you're talking to conservatives and you start talking about 'spread the wealth around.' That is tantamount to socialism."

In another e-mail obtained by Media Matters, Sammon told his staff to *downplay the importance of climate science* that showed the world was getting warmer.

Additional emails showed that Sammon asked his news department to refer to the public option as the "government-run option" because polls showed the phrase "government option" was opposed by the public.

I think what is the most important thing to note here is not only what he said, but also **where** he said it. He didn't say these things on MSNBC, or CBS, or in an interview in the *New York Times*, no. He went on **FoxNews** and said those things. He went on his own news network and intentionally pushed false facts and ideas in order to misinform. But then let's take one more step and ask, "Who is he trying to misinform?" Is it the liberals, or the Democrats, or some jerks from the government?

No.

He is purposely and intentionally misinforming **his own viewers**. He's is feeding false information to the people who turn to his news organization to get the facts and information. He's not lying to me, or to Nancy Pelosi, or Ralph Nader; he's lying to the people who trust him and his news organization to inform them on the important news items of the day.

To me, it is impossible to overstate just how important this is, and it certainly seems to be the point most often overlooked. Cuz for me that is what really distinguishes them from MSNBC. Fox News is parasitic on the worst instincts of its viewers; playing on their fears and insecurities, they create an irrational and endless resistance to anything mildly liberal or having to do with Barack Obama. The pursuit of truth is not their modus operandi, and there is no low to which they won't stoop to maintain their demographic.

I should note: as of the writing of this book, two years later, Bill Sammon still holds the post of Fox's Washington managing editor and vice president of the network. And no, Fox News has never been threatened by the FCC over this or any of its other horrifically partisan acts of malfeasance.

So, just to be clear, a television station in America is terrified of accidentally showing Janet Jackson's tit for two seconds, but they will happily slander and misinform without fear of consequences.

FALSE EQUIVALENCIES: SCARBOROUGH UNFAIR

Joe Scarborough: Every time you bring up Fox, you gotta bring up MSNBC.

Mika Brzezinski: I don't see MSNBC going after Democratic presidential candidates and trying to hire them . . . Roger Ailes gets behind Republican candidates and puts them on the air; it is a mouthpiece for the Republican Party.

Scarborough: I can't be quiet here; what do you think

MSNBC is at night? It is *exactly the same*!

Brzezinski: I don't think so.

Scarborough: Of course you don't, because you are a
   Democrat . . .

Yes, Joe nails this one. MSNBC and Fox News are exactly the same. I mean, if it weren't for MSNBC's mildly cerebral intellectualism, you wouldn't need to balance that out with Fox News' extreme, ignorant hate-mongering.

The only difference between them is that Bill O'Reilly exploits fear and racism, while Rachel Maddow uses logic and deductive reasoning to scare the shit out of racists who watch Bill O'Reilly.

But his response is surprise (false or sincere; either way he's a fuck ball). Obviously MSNBC does not speak with the loud and clear editorial voice that Fox does. Obviously MSNBC does not hire major operatives from directly within the Democratic Party. Obviously MSNBC does not act as one long infomercial for a political platform.

How do I know this? They hired Joe Scarborough and put him on camera for 15 hours a week. Every morning they kick off their day of liberal programming with 3 hours of nonstop talking points delivered to you by a panel of "familiar faces" made up of conservatives, Wall Street insiders, and the odd plagiarist.

What is bothersome about Scarborough in this case (as opposed to the myriad of other bothersome things in all other instances) is he constantly asks us to appreciate that he's able to think outside of any party affiliation. Though he doesn't demonstrate this ability with much frequency.

Unfortunately, without any party affiliation, he has no one to blame for his half-baked reactionary pronouncements but himself. Sean Hannity can always say, "Hey, don't blame me for that shitty racist stuff—I just say what they tell me and cash the checks." Mr. Scarborough must say, "Yes, that's something I thought of myself, and I am 100% responsible for how stupid it is."

Here is the heart of the False Equivalence: Fox News, and the Republican machines in general, put out demonstrably false talking points—in fact, they scream them—crafting them so any asshole can repeat them, which lets them think they understand an issue—then say it over and over again.

Hell, as we learned, Fox News executives have admitted to repeatedly pushing outright false information on their own news station.

When journalists actually do their jobs and deconstruct the logic, facts, or assumptions of these talking points, the right wing (and non-partisan people who have simply not given the matter any serious thought, but weigh in anyway) shout that it's "all the same thing," and therefore the world is fair, and they are not lying assholes.

Problem being, these are not two opposing positions or philosophies—unless you consider, say, snake oil advertisers and the FCC equal philosophical adversaries. To the idiots of the world, the fact that there *is* a dialectical conflict suggests that MSNBC and Fox News are like pugilists of the same weight class, when in fact, it is more like reasonable people trying to fight a herd of stampeding wildebeests.

This paradigm alone should tell Americans everything they need to know about the contemporary Republican Party. They think of people who *deal in facts* as an equal political opposition. The logical conclusion must be that the Republican Party is *against* the thing which most of us construct from factual information, i.e. *reality*.

I feel bad for Joe Scarborough . . . he's a lonely voice of conservatism in a vast wasteland of liberal news owned 49% by General Electric.

I would argue that MSNBC gives us as much "liberal" bias as can be stomached by banks, defense contractors, and media conglomerates.

See, that is who owns MSNBC and NBC—so they do all the hiring and firing over at Liberal TV News Land. And it appears to me that MSNBC's sole purpose is to make as much money off the Left as they can without doing any real damage to their corporate bottom line.

Whereas Fox News is a totally different kind of organization. As Mark Karlin has pointed out:

> **"The sole purpose of this emotional, incendiary, and deceptive narrative was to create governments that supported the plutocracy, not the 'rabble' of democracy. The tool to accomplish this was the manipulation of the mass media to ignore facts and create a fictional 'frame' that pushed populations toward acceptance of an authoritarian state, one that existed for the benefit of the wealthy."**

So yeah, they're exactly the same.

THE POOR HAVE IT TOO GOOD— SAY MILLIONAIRES

> Lou Dobbs: (The poor) have not only a microwave; they have an oven, they have a dishwasher, they have a dryer . . . Xboxes and PlayStations are in the homes of the typical family defined as poor.

> Bill O'Reilly: How can you be poor and have all this stuff? The Heritage Foundation came out with a study from six years ago that listed all the stuff poor people own in America—stuff like electrical appliances.

Fox News got a hold of the study, dusted it off, and had Bill O'Reilly and Lou Dobbs interpret it for us. And who better than those two callous millionaires to sit around telling us how good the poor have it. (I love the way Dobbs throws in Xboxes, as if it's a fact, when he just made it up, as there's no mention of Xboxes in the six-year-old, ultra-biased survey.)

Poverty ain't that bad, and the so-called poor are mostly a bunch of whiners. Always remember there's always reason when people are poor. That reason is that they basically aren't good people; they are irresponsible, and being poor is really a moral failing, like not working for Rupert Murdoch.

While quoting from the six-year-old survey from the Heritage Foundation, O'Reilly's voice rises whimsically every time he says "poverty". I shouldn't have to explain why that's not good journalism, especially since the economy fell apart three years ago when O'Reilly was saying this.

They mocked what an average worker's income is, yet these two rugged individualists wouldn't know how to survive on less than six figures a year, let alone $22K—and definitely not $22K with three dependents. Is there anything that resonates more with your sense of fairness than two out-of-touch millionaires sitting around telling poor people how good they have it?

"What I think this is all about is the underground economy; a lot of people that are reporting low wages are making a ton of money . . . "

The underground economy—did you hear that? These people who claim to be poor are all drug dealers—of course, that's not what they're *saying*, but if that's what you heard, who are we to correct you?

I think it's even worse that these supposedly poor people are all getting in on that cleaning houses pot o' gold—or some of the bling that comes from waitressing and migrant farm work. Fucking poor, always acting all poor when they're actually rich.

But wait! Bill O'Reilly makes an important point—people live in poverty because they are not personally responsible enough to go and get a job. But in 2011, when the economy was in the doldrums, there were no jobs—well, who's responsible for that? I'll tell you: The poor! If they would just take some responsibility and go get jobs, there would be more jobs in this country.

Free market capitalism doesn't create these problems, except when it's allowed to run completely unregulated and is able to purchase government policies—like now.

Dobbs and O'Reilly say that being poor inspires the innovators. Between these two guys, there has got to be at least forty pounds of balls, seeing as the biggest problem that small businesses (and those looking to start small businesses) are having is access to adequate short- and long-term credit from the free market capitalist system.

"If you're going to be poor, be poor in the United States," they say, laughing. This is what it's come to? We're better than Burundi, so shut up? Their message is: *Sure, more than 14% of the population is living in an inconceivable level or poverty—but they got TVs, so fuck 'em.*

They don't bother to figure out why poor people have access to electronics. Our consumerist society has encouraged a long and enormous consumer frenzy—which has put scads of secondhand appliances on the market.

"Thankfully the poor have cable so they can watch Fox," they joke. I don't think that's really a joke, so much as an inadvertent statement of how things work. The poor and uneducated will always watch TV—so we can continue to spoon-feed them this propaganda. If the poor start reading halfway decent newspapers, then these jokers are in serious trouble—if for no other reason than I've never seen a newspaper give a thinly veiled platform for people like the TeaBaggers and the Birthers to spout demonstrable falsehoods

THE WELL–TO–DO POOR?

"Bring in every poor person in America, and I can tell you why they're poor: They drop out of school, they get addicted to alcohol and drugs, they have a mental problem . . . there's always a reason in this country."
—Bill O'Reilly

He forgot *lazy*! Solved that one. What I love about O'Reilly is that he's not crazy like Glenn Beck, and he's not a provocateur like Rush Limbaugh, so you know when Bill O'Reilly says something, he really is a selfish, ignorant, narcissistic prick.

If you thought the sharp rise of poverty in America is because the system is rigged and getting an education bankrupts you, you're wrong. The poor are that way because they have a moral failing, just like Jesus said.

What if the poor didn't cause their own misery? What if bad things just happen to good people? What if everyone doesn't get what they deserve? Would it mean that God is cruel—or doesn't exist at all?

Well, that would mean that maybe Bill O'Reilly is just lucky, and that God doesn't actually favor hateful, unconscionable assholes. But now that Bill O'Reilly has told me how the world really works, it all just seems so simple, and I feel totally justified in every shitty thing I have ever done.

THE WAGES OF CNN

"Do the poor share responsibility for our economic woes?"
—Question of the day by CNN's Campbell Brown

Huh? That's the question of the day???? What questions did CNN reject?

"People with no money and no power, don't they deserve a kick in the teeth right now?" "Dressed a little too slutty? How much of the fault lies with the Rape victim?" "Are poor people gross?" "Setting homeless people on fire—is it wrong or just fun?"

> **"The poor actually have it better than the middle class. The poor live in decent houses and have refrigerators and microwave ovens, so what are they complaining about? Those are the people who pay the taxes in America, and the poor don't pay any! The president is the president of everybody; why focus on the poor?"**
> **—CNN's Carol Costello**

Yeah, why not focus on the rich? Everybody knows that, in a depression, they're the ones really hurting. Some of them can't even afford to heat the pools in their second homes anymore.

Carol Costello is asking this question to Tavis Smiley and Cornel West, who were promoting their "Poverty Tour," a road trip they embarked on to bring awareness to rising poverty in America and to give voice to those left out of the prosperity in our current economic system.

Seriously Carol, these are the guys whose feet you decide to hold to the fire? You let that weapons of mass destruction thing go unchallenged, the vilification of teachers, the repeal of banking regulations—but let's go hard on the least among us.

I have a few "questions" I'd like to ask Carol Costello. For example, "How many people on Wall Street do you think ought to be in jail over this?" Or how about, "How many people in the news media should lose their jobs for not warning us about the economic meltdown that I saw coming in 2005?"

No, she's worried about the fat cats at the bottom. Yeah Carol, I hear what you are saying—it's way easier to shit on poor people than it is to scrutinize the criminals at the top.

SURVIVING SEAN

"I have friends of mine that eat rice and beans all the time— beans, protein; rice, inexpensive. And you can make a big pot of this for a week, for relatively negligible amounts of money. . . . You should have vegetables and fruit in there as well, but . . . if you need to survive, you can survive off it . . . there are ways to live really, really cheaply."
—Sean Hannity, Fox News

He knows what he's talking about, because that's what he feeds his servants. "It's nothing fancy, but it sure beats a steady diet of my bullshit."

This shows how arrogant poor people are; they keep expecting to have fruits and vegetables.

Coincidentally, this is the very same diet that provides our Mexican neighbors with the nutrition they need to steal jobs from real Americans. "Yeah, I have plenty of other tips on living cheaply, too, like sleeping in your car and washing up at the Arco station."

Rice and beans taste even better after you've lost all hope. It's easy to eat when you're poor. It's much harder when you're wealthy and there's not enough time to eat everything. Maybe then next time you dumb bastards won't buy a house you can't afford to make the payments on.

CONFESSIONS OF A TV NEWS ADDICT

For the past dozen years or so, I've been paying attention to the news. As a comedian, I talk and write about the news. If there is one overriding theme which has emerged it is this: *The news is failing us.*

This truth—its dimensions and reasons—constitutes a book in itself. And man, oh man! That book would be funny and/or make me want to kill myself.

What I'm talking about here is the mainstream media: the large, supposedly reliable news outlets like the *New York Times,* CBS, CNN, etc. . . , Now, I should mention that the Right also has a problem with what Sarah Palin calls the "Lame-stream Media." However, Mrs. Palin and her cadre of nitwits tend to dislike the media when it is accurate and probing. You know, like when it asks "gotcha questions" like "What newspapers and magazines did you regularly read . . . to stay informed and understand the world?"

I, on the other hand, take issue with the mainstream media (or, as I call it, the "fucking mainstream media"), because they rarely ask any real "gotcha questions," like "Hey, isn't that yellow-cake uranium claim total fucking bullshit?" On that note, let's talk about something that really happened: David Gregory.

Now, David Gregory (or as I call him, "Fucking David Gregory") is the current host of NBC's *Meet the Press,* a position that once held great esteem and respect. Currently though, it is the *Arsenio Hall Show* of operatives peddling talking points like actors on a press junket. No statement can be too ridiculous, because everyone knows they will go unquestioned by host David Gregory. To be fair, I honestly think Arsenio would do a better job hosting *Meet the Press.* Here's one of the many telling quotes from Mr. Gregory, which should give you an idea of what I'm saying:

> **"I think there are a lot of critics who think that . . . if we did not stand up [in the run-up to the war] and say 'this is bogus, and you're a liar, and why are you doing this,' that we didn't do our job. I respectfully disagree. It's not our role."**
> **—NBC News' David Gregory, thereafter promoted to host *Meet the Press***

See, if they did that, it'd be "journalism." And that's not their role.

Then, what is their role? If the media defended Obamacare like they did the Iraq invasion, it'd have an 85% approval rating. I can see their dilemma: They can't search for the truth behind the rhetoric, because that'd make them look like Al-Jazeera.

Apparently, their role was to patriotically support the war until it became an unpopular disaster, and then disavow any moral responsibility for unpopular disasters. You see, in a democracy the press is not supposed to judge or criticize administration policy, kind of like the way the Russian media covered Khrushchev.

To be fair, if I were an overpaid network weasel, I would probably feel the same way. And let's face it, if you called every liar a "liar," pretty soon you'd be calling crooks "crooks," hypocrites "hypocrites," and war criminals "war criminals," and you'd end up on a cable channel nobody watches, like Dan Rather.

UP CHUCK

On the supposed more liberal MSNBC, Pennsylvania Governor Ed Rendell stated that most opponents of the Affordable Care Act have been fed erroneous information about the law. Chuck Todd said that Republicans "have successfully messaged against it," disagreeing with those who argue that the media should educate the public on the law.

> **"They don't repeat the other stuff because they haven't even heard the Democratic message. What I always love is people say, 'Well, it's you folks' fault in the media.' No, it's the president of the United States' fault for not selling it."**

Chuck Todd is currently the Chief White House Correspondent for NBC News and NBC News' political director. Seriously, the guy who said that has those jobs. Just so we're clear: It's not the media's job to let you know when one side is lying. It's the president's job. So if the GOP says the president is lying about Obamacare, all the president has to do is tell you he isn't. And then you know who to believe!

I mean, instead of being obsessed with what side's "messaging" (also known colloquially as "bullshit") is better, the media could look at the actual facts and report the actual truth. But if they were to do that and find out that one side is lying, they'd be in a real bind . . . because reporting as much would prove that they're biased (against liars).

Claims and facts are not equivalent. Facts tend to trump claims pretty well. The guy from the Americans for Prosperity think-tank who says, "there is no global warming" is not exactly the same as the scientist who says there is. By treating all this political hot air equally, the press is failing to present—forget the "fair and balanced" nonsense—an *accurate* picture of an issue. Without accurate information, the electorate simply cannot make informed decisions.

So, what I'm saying is this: if Chuck Todd is a shitty journalist— which he is—it endangers democracy as we know it. Someday I'll find a joke for that.

THE LIBERAL MEDIA MYTH

> "[Phil Donahue could be a] difficult public face for NBC in a time of war. . . . He seems to delight in presenting guests who are anti-war, anti-Bush, and skeptical of the administration's motives."
> —MSNBC memo on decision to fire Phil Donahue

> "We're all neo-cons now."
> —MSNBC's Chris Matthews, April 9, 2003

One of those guys was fired by the "liberal network." Which one would you guess? Was it the guy with the lower ratings? Hmmm, let's see.

In the run-up to the Iraq war, one of MSNBC's hosts was committed to giving a full airing to the critics and the criticisms of what soon became a horribly failed, illegal war for oil. The viewers rewarded him by making him the highest-rated show on the MSNBC network. MSNBC executives rewarded him for being the most-watched show on the network by . . . firing him.

Huh?

Yes. MSNBC executives publicly said they were getting rid of the show with the network's highest ratings because of "low ratings."

By "low ratings," they meant "high ratings by a liberal pacifist with integrity."

Makes sense. I'm sure it wasn't because MSNBC is owned by one of the most profitable defense contractors on earth? No, that's just how LIBERAL TV networks operate; when they are having ratings trouble, they get rid of the show with the highest ratings first, because they're liberals and *bad* at business, not because they are owned by the war machine that is *great* at business.

Isn't that just like the liberal media, to fire a true liberal and keep all the warmongering fake liberals at MSNBC just to throw us off?

I wonder what they told Donahue: "Sorry, Phil, but we're going in another direction. That way, where all the billion-dollar defense contracts are."

Phil's big mistake was doing his show as if there actually were freedom of the press, when everybody knows freedom of the press ended when the second plane hit the World Trade Center.

That really did happen. How do we know it was because Phil was anti-war? Well there was a memo from the MSNBC brass that was leaked that said Donahue would be a: "difficult public face for NBC in a time of war. . . . He seems to delight in presenting guests who are anti-war, anti-Bush, and skeptical of the administration's motives."

The report went on to argue that Donahue's show could become "a home for the liberal anti-war agenda at the same time that our competitors are waving the flag at every opportunity."

Interesting that NBC didn't question the flag-waving; they questioned questioning the flag-waving.

Obviously the executives at MSNBC thought it best in wartime to err on the side of becoming Fox News.

That's who MSNBC is, a corporate money-making machine that only cares about making money and not being liberal. If they can make money being pro-war, then let's do it; if they have to shut some liberals up to do it, no problem.

Good thing they got rid of him, too; who needs people who are right about an illegal war mucking up a defense contractor's thirst for war profits?

It all worked out anyway, because even though Phil Donahue was absolutely right and everybody who beat the drum for war was completely wrong, none of them ever admitted it, which is the same as being right all along.

Of course they kept Chris Matthews.

Matthews eventually switched sides and suppressed all the MSNBC footage that showed him cheerleading the invasion, which proves *1984* was a documentary.

"The bottom line is we need you, Phil [Donahue], because we need to be challenged by the voice of dissent."
–Oprah Winfrey to Phil Donohue after he was fired from MSNBC for his vocal opposition to the Iraq war.

She should have gone on to say, "But as far as network news goes, you're damaged goods, Phil, so enjoy your retirement, and say hi to Marlo Thomas for me."

Don't worry Rachel Maddow, your job is probably safe until President Cruz goes to war with Iran.

THE NEWS MEDIA IS LIBERAL!
(. . . and being brought to you by multinational corporations, defense contractors, and oil giants)

Turn on any Sunday news show, and it is 90% conservatives, corporate mouthpieces, or military people, fulfilling their Sunday morning pledge to give voice to the wealthy and powerful.

The media is corporate, not liberal; they serve the corporate interest first, last, and in the middle. The news is funded by advertisers, corporations like Wal-Mart, the drug companies, CitiGroup, and Boeing. Those are the people for whom the news is really prepared. Yes, the very people the newsman is supposed to be investigating are actually the ones funding his investigation. More accurately stated, they are funding the media's non-investigation. Banks, defense contractors, and multinational corporations pulling the purse strings of the news? Sounds like a regular liberal conspiratorial plot to me.

Yeah, but they've done studies that show most people in the news voted for the Democrat last election!

Oh sure, if you don't vote for an obvious lunatic, then that proves liberal bias. It never crosses their minds that maybe John McCain and Sarah Palin were horrible candidates? And ditto for Mitt Romney and Paul Ryan? *and* that maybe we take a cue from the voting habits of the most informed people in the country instead of dismiss them because it doesn't line up with uninformed opinions formed by internalizing corporate talking points constantly repeated and rarely debunked in the "LIBERAL" media?

Here is a typical Sunday news show panel getting ready to express views of the regular American citizen:

"Let's meet our powerhouse roundtable: George Will, Jonathan Karl, General Wesley Clark, Gwen Ifill, and Liz Cheney."
—Jake Tapper, host of ABC's *This Week*

So, that's:

- a conservative journalist,
- a conservative reporter,
- a guy from the Pentagon,
- an African-American ardent defender of the status quo (badly playing the role of liberal),
- and LIZ CHENEY!

Well, you could get a better cross-section of America if you didn't try. Sure, that's my voice—if my voice is that of a corporate stenographer, millionaire conservative, or a defense contractor. But if you are part of the other 95% of the American electorate, sit back and enjoy the commercials.

LIBERAL MEDIA PBS STYLE–MARK SHIELDS

". . . The fact is that the American people, who want all the benefits and want the free lunch, and don't want a single gray hair on the beautiful head of Social Security or Medicare touched, and basically don't want to pay for it . . ."
—Mark Shields, "Liberal" PBS commentator

Hey jackass, we do pay for it. It's called the payroll tax—FICA (Federal Insurance Contributions Act). And that was being said from someone supposedly representing the liberal side of the argument on PBS! I swear to Jesus, the next person who calls benefit programs that people have paid into over years of work a "free lunch," I'm going to do unspeakable things to that person with a heavy dictionary.

Fittingly, the term "No Free Lunch" comes from the "Great Depression" when bars could no longer provide a free lunch with drinks . . . except in this case, it would just be a "Great Depression" for the elderly.

> **". . . the old line is, we elect Republicans because we don't want to pay for it and we elect Democrats because we want everything that government is going to give us."**
> **—Mark Shields, dumbass**

How's about you don't say "we," OK? Because I, for one, know exactly what it might cost to pay for things. Now, if there are people out there who want all the benefits of government but don't understand they have to pay for it, well those people are called "fucking morons"—not "we."

And just as a side note: seems to me it was the Republicans who came up with the brilliant idea of cutting taxes to pay for TWO multi-trillion dollar wars.

> **". . . I would say there has been lack of leadership as far as sacrifice across the board. The White House, to the Congress, to our national leadership, to us in the press as well, I guess . . ."**
> **—Mark Shields, God shield us from this dope**

You guess there's been a failure of the press?! Dude, you just described Social Security as a "free lunch"—you're not failing in leadership; you're failing at factually describing phenomena.

"Failure of leadership" is a fashionable political term lately, which seems odd, since the Republican Congress has made it impossible to lead, even within their own party. Telling people to lead, then viciously resisting that leadership, is something you see on *Bridezillas*.

Three questions come to mind:

1. Does Mark Shields ever talk to a progressive Democrat?
2. Does Mark Shields maybe ever glance at a Paul Krugman column once in a while?
3. Does PBS think "liberal commentary" means "ideas slightly to the right of Joe Scarborough"?

I ask those questions because we are currently giving 60 to 80 *billion* dollars a month to the banks. It is called "quantitative easing." That's when the federal government takes 80 billion taxpayer dollars and, instead of spending it on teachers, cops, and firemen, or building roads, schools, and hospitals, they give it directly to the banks. We get nothing for it—not one person gets to see a doctor, or gets to pay a heating bill for an old person, or not one kid gets a meal when he goes to school. Nada. What we get is a lawsuit from AIG.

FYI: Social Security is *solvent* at least until 2033, and Medicare is running a surplus for the next 11 years.

That fact should be the starting basis for this discussion, or else it isn't very informed. And these are supposed to be the *informed smart people*. Not one mention of creating well-paying jobs here in America so we collect more taxes for these "Free Lunch" programs. Not a word about income disparity and the concentration of wealth at the top. No, Mark Shields says that we must not be afraid to tax the middle class? Holy shit.

Is Mark Shields too busy with PBS groupies that he can't learn the basic facts of the topic he's discussing?

AM I HEARING YOU *RIGHT?*

You would think that, if the free market really worked, half the talk stations would be right wing talk and the other half would be liberal talk, right? I mean, if the conservative theory that free markets meet every need and fix every problem, then that's how the radio dial should look, right?

But that's not what happens. Instead, the corporations that want to push a corporate agenda hire people who won't undermine it.

And who are those people? Right-wing maniacs, that's who. Rush Limbaugh, Mark Levin, Neal Boortz, Sean Hannity, Michael Savage, Glenn Beck, Dennis Miller, Laura Ingraham . . . that's quite a think tank.

A report on media ownership by the Center for American Progress revealed that, among radio formats, the combined news/talk format leads all others in terms of the total number of stations per format and trails only country music in terms of national audience share. Through more than 1,700 stations across the nation, the combined news/talk format is estimated to reach more than 50 million listeners each week, and conservative talk radio undeniably dominates the format.

The 257 news/talk stations owned by the top five commercial station companies reveal that 91% of the total weekday talk radio programming is conservative, and 9% is progressive.

Soooooo, why is this happening? Because that's what the market wants!

Really? The Los Angeles radio *market* wants 90% conservative talk? Hippie dippy, liberal Los Angeles? How can that be a function of what the market wants?

The fact of the matter is that media companies are no longer restricted from owning as many radio stations in any market as they want. There used to be a law against too much media ownership in any market; you couldn't own a newspaper and a radio station and a TV station in the same market. It was a good rule because it guaranteed diversity of opinion on the airwaves and a better informed and better served listener/viewer.

You know how the fox bought the hen house? Well, that fox owns the government that appoints the FCC board that reversed all those rules. Now our radios emit non-stop right wing talking points into our earholes.

How's that for your liberal media?

KURTZ–HEART OF DARKNESS

"Let's be candid, Jon Stewart appeals to you because he comes at his comedy and satire and criticism from a liberal point of view."
—Howard Kurtz, "media critic," completely missing the point

I hate to keep kicking a dead horse, but try reading this excerpt of an interview "media critic" Howard Kurtz did with Arianna Huffington, and tell me there is any hope for us. Keep in mind, Howard Kurtz is a media critic who departed CNN for repeatedly filing false stories. It didn't worry him because all those years of making false equivalencies between the Left and the Right paid off—he was quickly gobbled up and offered a job by that paragon of journalism: Fox News. Seriously, is there anything funnier than a "media critic" who works for Fox News? That's like making the winner of the Taco Bell burrito-slam contest a restaurant critic.

Here Kurtz keeps pushing the idea that there is no objective truth, that when someone is exposing hypocrisies and inconsistencies, he must be a liberal, and therefore we can dismiss it.

> **Howard Kurtz: Let's be candid, Jon Stewart appeals to you because he comes at his comedy and satire and criticism from a liberal point of view.**

> **Arianna Huffington: If you watch his interview with the president, he exposed the Achilles heel of the president; that's not cheerleading.**

Kurtz: . . . well no, he came off as a disappointed liberal. But let's leave that interview aside; when I see clips of the Daily Show on The Huffington Post, they tend to skewer conservative targets. You like that.

Huffington: . . . he uses satire to speak truth to power, whether it be liberal, conservative, in the media, in politics, that's where their power comes from, and those people who continue to see it as a "left-leaning show" are completely missing its appeal.

Kurtz: I think I disagree on that.

You see, in Howard Kurtz's world, there is only left and right; there cannot be honest journalism, or even accurate satire. Jon Stewart certainly doesn't need me defending him, but what Kurtz says is revealing of the media's heart of darkness. In Howard Kurtz's world, when Jon Stewart is skewering Republicans, he is just being a liberal partisan, and when he is skewering a Democrat he is just being a *disappointed* liberal partisan.

Now, I have issues a-plenty with Jon Stewart, and indeed with Arianna Huffington too, yet I would concede that currently the world would be worse without them around. But if Howard Kurtz disappeared tomorrow, the national discourse would not suffer an iota . . . in fact, it might not even notice.

FALSE EQUIVALENCIES: JOHN HEILEMANN

Let's get nostalgic and try to remember the presidential campaign we all worked hard at forgetting. Like many of you, the morning after the second presidential debate, I was being asked, "Hey, did you watch the debate last night?" To which I responded, "Of course, but did you watch all the assholes being paid to talk about it afterwards like they know a goddamned thing?"

And thus we come to John Heilemann on MSNBC sitting around a table with some other middle-aged white men, all getting paid to speculate wildly and give us exactly no new information. You know, the news.

You may remember John Heilemann as the journalist who wrote *Game Change*, the book that describes what an unreasonable idiot Sarah Palin is, but the people who chose her as a VP candidate were all super-smart people.

The way campaigns work in America is that the candidates are supposed to take a more extreme left or right position in the primaries to attract each party's respective base voter. But then the candidate moderates himself in the general election to appeal to the middle or the moderates in the electorate.

The shift Mitt Romney had to do in the last election from the primary to the general election was unprecedented. Here is John Heilemann saying what I had been saying for a long time, that Mitt Romney was running a campaign based almost completely on lying, and was making a complete mockery of the political process, the news media, and the American people—half of which Romney said he can't be bothered to think about.

John pushes back against Joe Scarborough's false equivalence about both candidates running toward the center in the general election:

> **"Joe, you are totally right, candidates from both parties go to extremes (in the primary) and then gradually drift back to the center . . ."**

True, if by both parties he means "one" party, and that would be the Republican Party. During the primaries of '08, the best you could say of any Democrat was that they went to the extreme left of the right wing . . . yeah, they were so far left in the '08 primary that one time they even mentioned that the environment might be a thing.

"What Governor Romney has done—it's really audacious what he's tried to do in this last month: to make the switch this late—"

"Audacious" implies that there was an actual consciousness behind his campaign. On the other hand, if you assume Mitt Romney is just a suit filled with ambition, then *all* the tiles fall into place much more neatly. In that instance, he's shifting positions late in the game because he's a liar and a moron, which would also explain . . . well, everything. It's like physics, really.

And then catch this little piece of journalistic sleight of hand John Heilemann lays on us, when he blames the president for the fact that Romney's complete duplicity and lies are going unchallenged in the campaign:

"We rightly criticize President Obama for not nailing him on that and being more aggressive and being more confrontational and holding his feet to the fire in the first debate in Denver; that was a large part of his failing, and so I guess the question for Chuck Todd is . . ."

I guess the question for Chuck Todd is "Can you believe the balls I have to call out Barack Obama for not doing *our* job!?"

Sure, their only duty, in fact their entire job, is to make sure that people are aware of what is happening in the world, and the biggest thing happening right then was that Mitt Romney was a complete fraud, and don't you think somebody should've been trying to convey that information to the American public? Like maybe a NEWS

PERSON or something. Oh, I can't wait for someone to invent newspapers and magazines and TV news shows so we will have institutions in place whose only purpose is to make sure the American electorate is aware of these things, and not just policy wonks.

Here is the actual question he asked Chuck Todd:

Heilemann:"Do you think it is too late? Is this a strategy that Mitt Romney can actually pull off? We've never seen a candidate tack to the center this fast this late in an election; can Pres. Obama impose a price on Mitt Romney for that? . . . Or is it possible that the 'audacity of etch' will work?"

Todd: "The president let him do it at the first debate, didn't call him on it."

First off, it's nice to know when Chuck Todd sees that a person who wants to be the next president is completely lying, Chuck crosses his fingers and hopes the opposing candidate calls him on it . . . because he's a newsman and powerless to do anything about it.

Secondly, what the fuck is Chuck Todd talking about?! Everyone has called him on it. The Democrats called him on it when he ran for Senate; the Republicans called him on it when he ran for president the first time; they called him on it when he ran for president this time. And for some goddamn reason, no one in the fourth estate wanted to stand up and say "This isn't a partisan thing; this guy is a liar. He's not a flip-flopper; he's a liar. His positions don't evolve; he doesn't soften them or sharpen them—he flat out changes them to suit his ambitions at that particular moment. He's pro-life, then he's pro-choice, now he's pro-life. He's for healthcare, now he's not. The man stands for absolutely nothing. He has no vision for America—he has no plan—he just wants to be president because he's gotten everything he's ever wanted in his life, and he feels entitled.

"And at the end of the day, no one seems to care. Republicans are so interested in winning that they've fallen in love with the guy they hated six months ago. Some Democrats are so petulant about their disappointment with Obama, that they don't see the dangers inherent in letting Chauncy Gardener here have his hand on the button. And somehow, there are about a million people left in this country who are engaged enough to say they are voting, but not engaged enough to have formed an opinion on a campaign that has been in the news cycle literally every day for the last year. God is dead. I hate you all." And . . . scene.

Something like that would have been nice.

CONVERSATION WITH A RUSTED ANCHOR

JIMMY DORE: Joining us now is legendary NBC newsman Tom Brokaw. I've got to ask, do you really think the generation you're always writing about was really the GREATEST generation?

TOM BROKAW: Jimmy, that's the generation that stormed the beaches at Normandy and made the world safe for democracy. With all due respect, the generations that came after are useless pieces of crap. People your age wouldn't understand that because your prostates are too small.

JIMMY DORE: But subsequent generations fought for civil rights, feminism, and marriage equality. Don't you have any praise for them?

TOM BROKAW: Oh, sure I do. All that civil rights and feminism stuff is just adorable. I'm more than willing to call them the "The Cutest Generation."

JIMMY DORE: Cute? Really?

TOM BROKAW: Yes, I'll be the first to admit that the troops who fought Hitler, for all their valor and bravery, never came up with any viral cat videos. This generation is tops in that department, no doubt about it.

JIMMY DORE: Mr. Brokaw, you are still very active in the world of broadcast journalism.

TOM BROKAW: That's right, Jimmy. I admit that I am getting on in years, but that hasn't diminished my passion for going into TV studios and pontificating thoughts of bland conventional wisdom. That's a journalistic fire that never leaves the belly.

JIMMY DORE: But if you don't mind my saying so, Mr. Brokaw, you are quite timid when it comes to holding politicians accountable for their actions.

TOM BROKAW: Jimmy, I'm not here to give you a lesson in Washington Journalism 101, but the first thing any reporter learns is never say anything about a politician that will make things awkward if you run into him or her at a Georgetown dinner party.

JIMMY DORE: Really? I never heard that . . .

TOM BROKAW: It's true! Jimmy, when we reporters are covering stories of national import, there is a lot at stake. When you interview or comment on a powerful figure, what you say and the way you say it has the potential to ruin an entire weekend on Martha's Vineyard.

JIMMY DORE: That doesn't seem very important to me.

TOM BROKAW: No? Well, let me paint you a little picture, Jimmy—just imagine yourself spending the whole morning riding a moped all over, looking for just the right Chardonnay to go with the gazpacho you've prepared for your casual power brunch. You put all this effort into making everything just right, and then Donald Rumsfeld spends the whole party sulking because he didn't like that someone on your broadcast said there were no weapons of mass destruction. Oh, there's mass destruction all right—of the delightful soirée you were hoping would be the hit of the social season! I've seen it happen, and it's something about which a responsible journalist should be ever vigilant.

JIMMY DORE: Mr. Brokaw, I'm sorry, but I just don't think you have your priorities straight.

TOM BROKAW: And that's why your generation sucks!

WHAT'S
WRONG
WITH
REPUBLICANS?

"It is a generalized massive branding problem."
—Joe Scarborough, MSNBC host and shitty detective,
explaining why people hate Republican policies

Researchers asked a series of questions about 23 major issues, aimed at ascertaining which political party's position people agree with. Turned out, from gun control to healthcare to abortion to unions, people agreed with the Democratic position on 22 of the 23 issues.

This prompted Joe Scarborough to respond that the problem is really just . . . branding. Really, Joe? We're talking about the modern- day Republican Party. It's not like you have the greatest chocolate bar in the world, and the problem is it's named "Cancer." The problem is you are selling the world's worst smelling lump of shit, and you think the problem is the wrapper.

No need to change your narrow-minded, reactionary positions on everything, you just have to "rebrand" yourself. Try some slick TV ads with dark people in them.

An easy way to change people's *perception* of who you are is to start changing your backward ideas on . . . everything. Except that 23rd thing.

But you're right about one thing, Joe . . . your problem is massive.

PHONE MESSAGE FOR JIMMY

JOHN BOEHNER

Jimmy? It's me, Boehner—(long, exasperated exhale)—Why in God's name did I want to be Speaker of the House? Oh, I remember: commanding a legion of rabid house cats wasn't available. I could be smoking, playing golf, and telling racist jokes right now, but noooooo . . . I had to make my dead father proud by captaining this goddamn Titanic straight to the port of Fuck-me-istan.

On one side, I got the Tea Party people—"Hey, we came to Congress specifically not to govern!" What the hell is that? "Hey, I tried out for the basketball team specifically so I could refuse to play basketball." These people informally appointed Crazy Eyes Bachmann their leader—if you're gonna do that, why not just put a pig head on a stick and worship that? Then, I got Canter breathing down my back—hey Eric, since you're always back there anyway, why not massage my hemorrhoids while you're at it? Man, that guy is six kinds of creepy. I make sure I am never alone with him, let alone make eye contact. He's always like, "Hey John . . . you want a piece of candy from my pocket?"

Then I got Norquist—fucking Norquist. "If you raise taxes, I'll find someone more to the right to challenge you in your next primary!" Really? You're gonna find someone further to the right of Peter King? Well, good luck travelling to the underworld to find that guy.

Jimmy, I'm telling you, I am surrounded by so many defectives, I can't even cry at public speaking events anymore—and that was my thing, man—that was like, my signature move. I would mention the 'rents, cry like a giant orange baby, then I was out.

I'm just venting, man—cuz ugh.

OK, I am gonna go, but Jimmy, I am going to imagine you are giving me a long, manly, gentle hug. Like you just took me in your weird, bony arms and let me smell your scent, and—

(lump in throat)

Oh—there, now the tears are finally coming—I gotta get to a microphone!

(BEEP)

THE RIGHT WING ALMANAC WITH GARRISON KRISTOL

And here is the Right Wing Almanac for Thursday. It was on this day in 2000 that the U.S. Supreme Court in a five-to-four decision issued an order halting the recount of contested ballots in Florida, thereby giving the election to George W. Bush, though Al Gore likely won the election. Alan Dershowitz called the order ". . . the single most corrupt decision in Supreme Court history."

And we were then plunged into eight years of darkness where

the beast ruled the world through the currency of ignorance.

It's the anniversary of Senior White House Advisor Edwin Meese saying, in 1983, that people went to soup kitchens "because food is free and that's easier than paying for it." Two years later, Meese would say that he didn't believe Miranda warnings were necessary, because "you don't have many suspects that are innocent of a crime." Naturally, in 1985, President Reagan appointed this Teddy Bear of Compassion to be U.S. Attorney General. True to form, Meese later resigned in disgrace when he was linked to fraudulent no-bid government contracts. As with all criminals and failures in the Republican Party, he has continued to play a prominent role in politics and business. Among other things Meese was recently the chairman of the Heritage Foundation—the league of evil that brought you the Iraq war—and is currently sabotaging the Strategic Arms Reduction Treaty.

Finally, it was on this day in 1958 that a group of completely insane and angry white men held their first meeting as The John Birch Society in Indianapolis, Indiana. Robert Welch Jr., a retired candy manufacturer, led the group of twelve that would eventually become one of the most influential right-wing cabals in America. Staunch anti-communists, even long after the Cold War, Society members find communist conspiracies in pretty much everything they don't like. For instance that show on NBC that everyone says is really funny, but I don't get it, so I feel bad, and they must be pinkos! The John Birch Society has opposed, among other things, the United Nations, civil rights, and the Occupational Safety and Health Administration. Also, they hate help—like basic helping of people—like they'll shout things like, "Hey Grandma, take some responsibility and walk yourself across the street!" or "Hold the door for you? What is this, Russia? Get out your own keys, comrade!"

Here are a few words for today by former President George W. Bush, perhaps apropos for this week: "We need to counter the shockwave of the Evildoer by having individual rate cuts accelerated and by thinking about tax rebates."

Be well, work it real good, and keep touching yourself.

DOWD IN THE MOUTH

Former Bush administration official Matthew Dowd is giving his advice on what he thinks the Republican Party should be doing to get back to relevance:

> **"They have to . . . run against Wall Street and run against Washington; they have to become the party of the middle class."**
> **—Matthew Dowd, on what Republicans need to do**

Really? Republicans need to "run against Wall Street and become the party of the middle class."

You mean become Democrats? They could use the help.

What would be the point of being a Republican? And what in the world is going to happen to the super rich without a voice in government?! Becoming the party of the middle class won't be easy after thirty years of policies that have eroded the middle class.

He says the Republicans need to let the people know they are different, and then says:

> **"I think they need to stake out a ground that basically says, we not only look different, we're gonna say things different . . . and whether they look at Marco Rubio, or Gov. Christie, looks different than normal people look, their brand has to change if they are going to win elections."**

Did he just say that Chris Christie doesn't look like a Normal Person?

It's all relative . . . compared to Haley Barbour, Chris Christie looks like George Clooney. I say Republicans need to lower their standards . . . they just lost with a guy that looked like Robert Stack. Chris Christie's candidacy would break down the doors of discrimination if he could only squeeze through them.

I'm sure Republicans will warm up to Marco Rubio, right after Bobby Jindal gets in the race.

WHITES ONLY

"What Republicans need to do to re-group, we'll ask our Sunday Panel."
—Chris Wallace (the bad Wallace), Fox News

"Republicans look to regroup," and by that he means to find ways to attract minorities to the Republican Party. Who better to figure out how to attract minorities than five of the whitest people in America: Evan Bayhe, Bill Kristol, Laura Ingraham, Kirsten Powers, and Chris Wallace. That was seriously who Fox News had on the panel to bring their revelatory perspectives on the matter. How about stop being the political party that seeks insights about minorities from the likes of Evan Bayhe, Bill Kristol, Laura Ingraham, etc . . . .

LOWER LEARNING

"We will never have the smart people on
our side."
    —Rick Santorum

He's right, those elite, smart, college-educated people will always be
against the conservatives, because they read books, and right-wingers
want to burn them.

> "President Obama once said he wants everyone in America
> to go to college, what a snob!"
>   —Rick Santorum (MBA, University of Pittsburgh)

OK, first thing: I'm pretty sure President Obama never said that.
I'm guessing he said he wanted everyone to be able to go to college.
Which isn't just a slight difference—it's completely different. And
also, this from the guy who wants everyone to get with the Lord. I,
for one, would rather sit through a state-mandated English survey
course than catechism—and that's not snobbery—that's a reasonable
sense of entertainment value.

"What a snob!"

Wow, how often do you hear someone hit a talking point that
hard?! I mean, he just said it. Man, at this rate, expect Santorum to
say "uppity colored fella" sometime soon.

Just as a point of logic—a true snob wouldn't want people to go to
college. They'd want the masses to stay ignorant so they could feel
superior to them . . . or exploit them, you know, like Foster Friess. Wait
. . . something just clicked in my head . . . nope, I lost it.

"There are good, decent men and women, who go out and work hard every day, and put their skills to test, that aren't taught by some liberal college professor that tried to indoctrinate them."

Hmm, it sounds like he's saying people who don't go to college and work really hard are somehow more "real" than the lazy slackers who go to college, and "phone in" the rest of their lives. He's almost saying there's a sort of social hierarchy . . . like, I don't know, a class warfare or something.

Indoctrinate them? What do Republicans think, that higher education is like a series of rituals in which the illogical dogma of a power structure is driven into the minds of young people? Like Sunday school, confirmation, first communion, mass, and confession?

"Oh, I understand why he wants you to go to college. He wants to remake you in his image!"

He does?!! He wants to remake me into the leader of the free world? What a fucking nightmare that would be! Oh wait, do you think Santorum means black? Like college turns you black? Man, that would be weird.

"You encouraged your kids to go to college?"

"I encouraged my kids to get higher education; absolutely, and in fact, if college is the best place for them, absolutely. But, you know what, if going to a trade school, and learning to be a carpenter or a plumber or other types of, other types of skills— an artist—whatever the case may be—"

Really, Rick? You'd be OK with your kids being artists? I am 100% sure that's not true, unless your kid wanted to paint Jesus a lot—or become the next Thomas Kincaid, the master of light. Oh, and by the way, most art schools are four-year colleges.

But, this guy has a point: remember all those Obama speeches where he shits on plumbers and carpenters? Remember how he wanted to get them all healthcare—yeah—the healthcare of judgment!

"—or musician—"

Rick, on behalf of everyone in the liberal community, I can honestly say, we would love for your kid to become a musician—cuz I guarantee that would not be an Osmond / Von Trapp family scenario. That would be a series of cocaine-fueled albums about what a repressed dick the old man is, ending with death by autoerotic asphyxiation.

"All of those things are very important and worthwhile professions that we should not look down our noses at, and say they are somehow less because you didn't get a four-year college degree . . ."

And really the best way to honor those professions is to defund every entitlement program that benefits working-class Americans we can get our hands on—oh, and, while we're at it—fuck the arts, too.

So remember, kids—don't listen to that elitist black asshole and go to one or more years of higher education (which is what Obama actually suggested). Just run with your high school diploma, which tells people you are a hard-working American—because you have no choice but to work at manufacturing jobs that no longer exist.

And don't worry about Social Security, because between your poverty and lack of healthcare, you'll die at forty or so . . . the way God intended. Because, there's nothing wrong with letting your intellectual insecurities rule your politics and life . . . unless you want to live.

But this isn't just about Rick Santorum; he is emblematic of a Republican Party that fears knowledge and book learning and shuns those who seek it.

This suspicion of higher learning does not sound unfamiliar coming from a modern-day Republican. Is there a day that goes by without a report of yet another elected Republican on tape denouncing evolution, or climate change, or science in general?

It didn't used to be this way. This is the party that used to brag about its intellectuals because it had real ones, and it held up thinkers like William Buckley as its standard bearer. Men who not only read books, but also wrote them. That used to be the Republican Party.

Now it is an unseemly gaggle of proud anti-intellectuals and religious zealots who tell their kids that college is hippie indoctrination as often as they shame their naughty parts. Try to find a bona fide modern-day conservative intellectual who hasn't been thrown out of the party yet.

David Frum, who had the temerity to suggest that the Republicans needed to compromise on Obamacare instead of offering nothing and losing, was fired from his post at the Heritage Foundation. The guy who coined the phrase "axis of evil" is too thinky for today's Republicans.

They are being run by radical morons—Bachmann, Palin, Gohmert, Santorum—a group that is trying to gain a majority in government by appealing to an even dumber group of people than themselves.

Who are today's conservative thinkers, the book writers that modern-day Republicans look to for guidance and ideas? Intellectual giants like Ann Coulter, Glenn Beck, and Mark Levin.

For a few months in the run up to the 2012 election, the Republican standard bearer was Herman Cain, who opened a speech thusly:

"[America] needs a leader, not a reader."
   —Herman Cain, said while the Republican presidential front-runner

That should scare them more than it does me.

PHONE CALL FROM RICK SANTORUM'S SWEATER VEST

Hi ho, Jimmireeno, it's me, Rick Santorum's sweater vest! Ricky darling keeps talking about running for president again; he even talks about it in his sleep. I thought I'd give the public a little peek into what it's like to be the sweater vest of a hearty hunk of a man like Rick Santorum!

I mean, some people have wondered, why would a man who wants to convey a sense of strength and leadership wear a sweater vest? I guess Rick decided that leather ass-less chaps weren't masculine enough for him. But it's all part of Rick's sly, subversive strategy to make hateful attacks against homosexuals while wearing a piece of clothing from the Jim J. Bullock Collection of Men's Fashions.

But as a sweater vest, I do more than make Rick Santorum look like a dweeb. I'm a very practical garment. When you're Rick Santorum and you spend all day being a gay-bashing, woman-hating, race-baiting fear monger, you don't want your bigoted intolerance weighted down by sleeves. Your arms can get very sweaty when you spend as much time pointing your finger in judgment as Rick does.

I've gotten to know Rick very well, because, frankly, he never takes me off. Ever! Maybe I shouldn't tell you this, but at night, Rick removes all of his clothing except for me. He finds me very sensual. He likes the way I make his flesh feel all tingly when I wrap myself around his skin. The truth is, he's a trans-vest-ual. But there's nothing sick or twisted about it! He doesn't use me for intercourse, because it's not a man's place to insert himself into a woman's vagina—that's the government's job!

No, Ricky prefers to look at himself in the bathroom mirror while slowly rubbing a Bible against me. And I'll have you know that he considers every sperm that he ejaculates all over the toilet seat cover to be a living, breathing human being, deserving of protection by the Personhood Amendment.

Well, I've probably revealed a little bit too much. I'd better be going. Rick just bought himself a fanny pack, and to be honest I'm a little worried. I feel that my status as the wussiest thing in Rick's wardrobe is threatened.

So long, Jimmy. Stay fabulous!

SORE LOSERS

"It's a changing country. There are 50% of the voting public who want stuff, they want things. And who is going to give them things? President Obama. . . . Twenty years ago, President Obama would be roundly defeated by an establishment candidate like Mitt Romney. The white establishment is now the minority."

—Bill O'Reilly, freaking out after Obama's win

They want *stuff* and *things*? I have to admit, he's got a point. The people who voted for Obama certainly want *stuff* and *things*.

For example they want *stuff* like: affordable healthcare, equal rights for gays, and equal pay for women. That kind of *stuff*.

But they are such leeches they also want things! Yep, things like: the right for women to make their own reproductive health choices, and a chance to earn a living at a decent job that won't be outsourced to a slave.

Things like freedom FROM religion, and a Federal Emergency Management Agency that actually can manage federal emergencies and natural disasters.

That would be the *stuff* and *things* that they want.

> **"The president succeeded by *suppressing the vote* . . . they effectively denigrated Mitt Romney's character, his business acumen, business experience."**
> **–Karl Rove, badly trying to seem victimized after losing to the black guy for a second time**

Let me explain what Rove means. "Suppressing the vote" is what happens when the other guy beats your guy decisively, and you look like an asshole.

Obama's campaign said terrible things about Romney, such as he's a rich guy who only cares about himself . . . and telling the truth like that is really out of bounds.

> **"They decided they are going to have this negative personal campaign to try to convince people that Romney was a bad person . . . they said he was a vulture capitalist— he was a bonfire bureaucrat married to an equestrian."**
> **–Haley Barbour**

See, you should feel sorry for Mitt Romney and the Republicans because Obama waged a negative personal campaign, just what you'd expect from a Kenyan Muslim socialist Manchurian candidate trying to destroy Christianity.

He is right when he says that Obama's outrageous attacks had nothing to do with Romney's true character, because Romney doesn't even have any character.

Funny to see the bullies cry that Obama's attacks were *personal*, which they were. Like the attack that Romney was *personally* going to overturn Roe v. Wade, end Medicare, and cut taxes for billionaires.

HEY, ASSHOLE!—CHRIS CHRISTIE

Following the 2013 death of New Jersey Senator Frank Lautenberg, Governor Christie decided to hold a special election for the seat, instead of the regular scheduled election the following month. It was obvious to everyone that Christie was doing this to confuse and obstruct the vote for popular Democratic challenger Cory Booker.

JIMMY DORE: Governor Chris Christie, I know you're in trouble for what you did with the Washington Bridge and withholding funds for Hoboken. It reminds me of when you decided to call a special election to fill a Senate seat.

CHRIS CHRISTIE: Yeah, what about it?

JIMMY DORE: Why not just have it on the same day as the regular election in November when you're on the ballot, too? I'm trying to figure why you do things the way you do. Now I want you to be honest. Why'd you do this?

CHRIS CHRISTIE: Just reminding people I'm a big fat douchebag. Plus, it's what we all deserved.

JIMMY DORE: What do you mean?

CHRIS CHRISTIE: The people of New Jersey deserve the senator, and I deserve to win my race for governor by 20 percent of the votes.

JIMMY DORE: Why do that and catch all this grief, that's my question. I mean you could have just had the election on the same day, and you still could have won the governor race by at least ten points . . . why do it this way?

CHRIS CHRISTIE: And I deserve to win by twenty points.

JIMMY DORE: Okay.

CHRIS CHRISTIE: That's who I am. I do things big. I don't eat 'til I'm full. I eat 'til I'm tired. I could have stopped eating after a few of those White Castles, but I finished a full gross and a half because it's who I am.

JIMMY DORE: Okay, but aren't you worried this move reveals you as the typical politician putting self-interest before civic duty?

CHRIS CHRISTIE: No, I ain't worried—people love it.

JIMMY DORE: What? What do you mean? People love it when you waste public money? That doesn't make any sense, Governor.

CHRIS CHRISTIE: No? Well people love it when I'm ballsy for no reason and act like I don't give a shit what people think of me. It's actually a very interesting phenomenon.

JIMMY DORE: You mean it's like when you're talking like a macho tough guy, even though it's obvious you're acting in your own self-interest and are wasting taxpayer money . . . you're telling me that people actually like that?

CHRIS CHRISTIE: Like it? *They love it.*

JIMMY DORE: Why?

CHRIS CHRISTIE: I'm not really sure. I have a few theories.

JIMMY DORE: Like what? Share them with me.

CHRIS CHRISTIE: Well, like, deep down, people generally hate other people. And when someone is being a dick to someone who is not themselves, they find it entertaining. Most people are pussies. It's a thing they wished they could do . . . would do . . . if they only had the balls and could afford to lose their shitty mizzzz-er-able jobs.

JIMMY DORE: Okay. I get it. That makes sense, watching you tell someone off, consequences be damned, the people are getting a little bit of a feeling of having done it themselves. Is that what you're saying?

CHRIS CHRISTIE: It's called a "vicarious thrill."

JIMMY DORE: Huh? What did you say?

CHRIS CHRISTIE: What you're describing is called "vicarious."

JIMMY DORE: Yeah, I know what vicarious means . . .

CHRIS CHRISTIE: Oh really, is that why you didn't say it?

JIMMY DORE: Governor, I'm familiar with the term "vicarous."

CHRIS CHRISTIE: Oh, but too bad your mouth couldn't be as familiar with it as you are . . . It's a real shame. My mouth is very familiar with that term. Which is why I said it.

JIMMY DORE: Okay, that's enough, let's move on.

CHRIS CHRISTIE: See, a bunch of people just got off on that!

JIMMY DORE: Got off on what?

CHRIS CHRISTIE: On me busting your stugots right now. That's right in front of your face. That's all.

JIMMY DORE: What?

CHRIS CHRISTIE: Sta-goon.

JIMMY DORE: What?

CHRIS CHRISTIE: People loved it cuz I was giving it back to you.

JIMMY DORE: That was stupid, though.

CHRIS CHRISTIE: Doesn't matter. Doesn't even matter that I'm wrong. All I've gotta do is be an ass, and some schmuck is going to eat it up; people eat it up. I can't deny it, it's fucking great.

JIMMY DORE: Okay. I can't deny that you have one of the highest popularity ratings.

CHRIS CHRISTIE: Nobody and nothing gets a 75% approval rating. I'm as popular as pizza and titties.

JIMMY DORE: Have you always known you've had this power?

CHRIS CHRISTIE: No, I first realized I had this power when way back I was doing this call-in show. This woman called in to bust my balls about cutting funding for public education. She asked me if I sent my kids to private school while at the same time cutting funding for public schools. Which was completely legitimate and a great point. I didn't know what to do.

JIMMY DORE: So what did you do in that situation?

CHRIS CHRISTIE: I thought to myself—if this is what it's like to be governor, getting bitched out by a pesky woman . . . and the public holds me accountable for my actions, then I don't want any part of it. And right then and there I decided to chuck it.

JIMMY DORE: What do you mean by chuck? Chuck what?

CHRIS CHRISTIE: . . . Being governor. I didn't want it any-more. So I told that broad to shut her fat mouth. It's none of her business where I send my kids to school, and a bunch of rude, inappropriate stuff.

JIMMY DORE: Yeah, you know what, I do remember that. That's kind of what made you famous, right?

CHRIS CHRISTIE: I thought for sure I was done. The people would be outraged by my behavior. And I could go back to my life screwing over the poor and working people in the private sector. But instead, they loved it. Which proves that most people in New Jersey are, deep down, hateful pricks who root for a bully. It's like a parallel universe. I could not be luckier.

JIMMY DORE: So that's when you realized that . . . you had this power?

CHRIS CHRISTIE: Yeah. And I tried to see how far I could push it? . . . Just how powerful my power is.

JIMMY DORE: Yeah, what did you do?

CHRIS CHRISTIE: The next thing I did was publicly demonize and bully a teacher. She was bitching about me cutting public education and cutting teachers' pay . . . you know, the usual B.S.

JIMMY DORE: Yeah, what did you do? How did you handle it?

CHRIS CHRISTIE: Oh I went *full asshole* on her. I told her we didn't need greedy teachers like her in New Jersey and to quit it if she didn't like it! I thought it would cost me the governor's mansion on that one. But it didn't. The stupid, hateful schmucks loved me even more. That's when news people started to like me publicly, too. And I knew that I had a true gift.

JIMMY DORE: And?

CHRIS CHRISTIE: And I decided to see just how powerful I

was. And I publicly called a Navy war veteran an idiot and had him removed from a public forum. I was really out of line. I mean, come on.

JIMMY DORE: And what happened?

CHRIS CHRISTIE: *People fucking loved it!!* Are you kidding me!? After that, Brian Williams and Brokaw invited me to join the "regular people's haters club." It was really a great day.

JIMMY DORE: Wow. That's an amazing gift you have or a power that people like. I don't get it.

CHRIS CHRISTIE: Yeah it's pretty great. I kicked some little boy in the nuts for no reason.

JIMMY DORE: What?

CHRIS CHRISTIE: They carried me out up on a shield.

JIMMY DORE: Okay.

CHRIS CHRISTIE: It took like eighteen guys, but you know, whatever.

JIMMY DORE: Well, Governor, I appreciate—

CHRIS CHRISTIE: Yeah, I've had a long day of beating up the little guy here, so I better get going.

JIMMY DORE: Yes. Well I appreciate you taking the time . . . but I want you to know that people are starting to see through you, and that it's going to be tough to become president. But thanks for taking time with us today.

CHRIS CHRISTIE: Hey, yeah. Guess what?

JIMMY DORE: Tell me.

CHRIS CHRISTIE: Fuck you.

IGNORANCE IS A VIRTUE

"Very rarely do I read a newspaper."
–John Kasich, Republican governor of Ohio

Wow! What was the question? Governor, why are you so shitty at your job? And why do you seem totally tone deaf to reality?
No that was Ohio Gov. John Kasich blaming the media for the passage of the referendum that repealed his anti-union legislation. He puts a new twist on the old phrase, "Reading is Fundamental"—now it's, "Reading is Peripheral."

But this does help explain why so many Republican ideals are more in line with comic books than newspapers . . . to them, Al Gore is the Green Goblin, Bill Clinton is the Joker, and Obama is Blade.

Lucky for us, Governor Kasich had even more to say on the subject:

"Very rarely do I read a newspaper, because just like some presidents have done in the past [I've found that] reading newspapers does not give you an uplifting experience. . . . Time to time, people will send me articles, and things I need to know about . . . My life's a lot better if I don't get aggravated by what I read in the newspaper . . ."

Okay, let's hold our nose and unpack that.

Yes, that's true, several presidents have chosen not to read newspapers – several truly terrible presidents. George Bush should not be your intellectual role model.

"[I've found that] reading newspapers does not give you an uplifting experience."

Wow, I never thought about it that way. I thought a newspaper was there to report useful information that someone like me, or maybe the *governor of a state*, might find useful. I didn't realize a newspaper was there to *uplift* me, like a sermon or a Kate Hudson movie.

"Time to time, people will send me articles, and things I need to know about."

Time to time? Don't you have daily meetings with advisors? Or are they also forbidden from delivering any actual information that might not uplift you? Are most of your staff meetings about gossip and planning office birthday parties?

He, one of the most powerful governors in the U.S., said he receives his news in the same manner and frequency with which he gets links to puppy videos on YouTube. Think it ever occurred to him this might have something to do with the failure of his legislative agenda?

"My life's a lot better if I don't get aggravated by what I read in the newspaper . . ."

And I'm sure the people of Ohio are grateful that your life is better. I'm sure they're sitting around going, "I'm out of work, the schools are screwed, I can't afford healthcare, and organized labor just took its worst body blow in 100 years—but the governor sure seems relaxed and easygoing."

Still, you gotta admit, he makes it really tempting to be a Republican. I mean, where else can you proclaim things that should be shameful and get rewarded for it? This guy just proclaimed he doesn't read the news, and his base is probably cheering. Our last president thought the world is six thousand years old, and he got elected twice! Don't you wish you could do that? "I'm a chronic masturbator, and I'm afraid a monster might live in my closet!"

"Here's a major position of power for you!"

But let's remember exactly who Johnny Genius is anyway.

He's a guy who was raised Catholic, but converted to Evangelical Christianity to be *more* conservative. Governor Kasich is currently hard at work fighting for the minorities in his state. And by minority, I mean the 3% of Ohioans who control the majority of that state's wealth. And he's fighting hard for those poor people by cutting corporate taxes and busting those bully unions—damn unions! Always trying to oppress the wealthy!

HEY, ASSHOLE!—JUDGE NAPOLITANO

"It is the height of stupidity to extend unemployment benefits; Americans need to get back to work!"
—Judge Napolitano, Fox Business

"The height of stupidity to extend unemployment benefits"?! Really, man? Even if it's stupid—a suggestion with which most economists would disagree—I hardly think it's the height.

I can think of a dozen things that are closer to the top of the stupid list—multiple tax cuts for millionaires, denying global warming, refusing to regulate an economy that just fell apart . . . but extending unemployment benefits? Most economists consistently say that unemployment is the fastest, most direct way to stimulate the economy. It occurs to me that the height of stupidity is to stand by your Horatio Alger dogma when all the empirical evidence is against you.

"Americans need to get back to work!"?!

Well, thank God someone said it. Hear that, you lazy sacks of trash who used to work but managed to get yourselves laid-off or fired?! The vacation is over—you know, the vacation in which you don't go anywhere relaxing, but instead stay home and worry all the time?

"The problem with unemployment benefits is that they encourage people not to take jobs, and they take money from the productive sector and give it to the unproductive. As I've said again and again, if you subsidize something, you get more of it; subsidizing unemployment leads to more unemployment."

Get back to work, you bunch of babies! Because these unemployment benefits are "encouraging people not to take jobs"! Do you hear me! The jobs are out there—despite all the evidence to the contrary, there are jobs—you people would just rather nap all day and suck on that sweet, sweet, below-the-poverty-line money.

It "take[s] money from the productive sector and give[s] it to the unproductive"?! Hold on, let me change that, cuz we've upheld all kinds of tax cuts for the wealthy and corporations—so, it takes money from nowhere and gives it to unproductive people.

Yeah, I know, it's weird. You'd think the only way our economy would work would be by taxing people an appropriate amount, and then spending that money for the good of the whole society—but it turns out the mechanics are, we tax no one and somehow pay for two wars. Why weren't we doing this all along?!

I'm just saying, "if you subsidize something, you get more of it."

For instance, we have been subsidizing defense contractors for years, and we are always getting more defense stuff—like in the next few years, we're getting thirty new $1.8 billion nuclear submarines, and next year we're going to spend almost $10 billion on missile defense, if we can just sabotage the ratification of the next nuclear treaty with Monaco.

Oh, also, we subsidize oil, and we just keep getting more and more of that—case proven, am I right!?! God bless Ronald Reagan!

RACISM IS OVER!
(unless you are black, Hispanic, or otherwise dark-skinned)

"I wish President Obama would learn how to be an American."
–John Sununu

Race baiting, it's not just for breakfast anymore. Always great when a guy born in Cuba to Arab parents starts yelling about who is sufficiently American.

Barack Obama, black kid born to a single mom, who worked his way through college, doesn't understand how America works. But you know who does? Mitt Romney! Yes, the guy who has never, ever bought groceries for himself and has a wife who teaches horses to dance.

Remember how Mitt Romney pulled himself up from the bootstraps hanging from his trust fund? Just when is Obama gonna open a Swiss bank account and marry a woman who teaches horses to DANCE?

"He has no idea how the American system functions. . . . He spent the early years in Hawaii smoking something. . . . and . . . he worked as a community organizer. . . . There has been no experience in his life in which he's earned a private sector paycheck that meant anything."

Yeah, if only Obama hadn't wasted his time graduating from Harvard and teaching law, he might've learned something about how America functions. While Obama was busy smoking weed and daydreaming, George W. Bush was honing his entrepreneurial skills by snorting coke. And what's community organizing anyway, besides helping black people to vote?

Hey Mr. Sununu, you know who else never earned a private sector paycheck? *Dwight Eisenhower.*

This thinly veiled racist tirade did not go unnoticed by the Oxy-Contin king of the a.m. dial.

> **"The only thing he [Sununu] left out was that Obama has been mentored, educated, bent, and shaped by a bunch of communists."**
> **—Rush Limbaugh**

I get it Rush, Obama was mentored, bent, and shaped by a bunch of communists—you know, at Harvard Law School, where Mitt Romney went.

I can see why they are freaking out; you just wait, since this America-hating socialist got re-elected, you won't even recognize this country in a few years, what with its slightly fairer tax code and people seeing doctors when they get sick.

If I didn't see the videos of them saying this stuff myself, I would think these were cartoons written to make them look like buffoons. But I did see the video, and they seem to be lacking the shame gene. Or the part of the brain that feels normal humiliation.

> **"I think it can be said WITHOUT EQUIVOCATION, without equivocation, this man hates this country."**
> **—Rush Limbaugh on President Obama**

Let's do a quick comparison: President Obama, who hates America, tried to get all Americans healthcare. Rush Limbaugh, who presumably loves this country, told poor children that they should learn to find food in dumpsters. See, Rush loves his country too, but it's in more of a "tough love" kind of way.

I love the way he keeps saying "without equivocation!" as opposed to all that equivocation he normally does. Cuz, you know, Rush is always saying, "To be fair, here's the other side of the argument."

HEY, ASSHOLE!–MICHAEL BLOOMBERG

"The reason it's so big [New York's income gap] is at that higher end, we've been able to do something that none of these other cities can do. And that is attract a lot of the very wealthy."
–Mayor Michael Bloomberg

The good mayor said this in response to a fresh report showing that New York City's income gap and poverty rate has grown during his tenure. In fact, NYC's income gap is wider than any of the other 30 major cities in the United States. Somehow, Bloomberg of the Shire is able to spin this in his head from a negative into a positive—you know, the way a sociopath might.

Yes, the reason the gap is so great is that all of the super wealthy want to live here, which is necessarily good . . . why? To be fair, the uber-wealthy are nice to look at, and they smell like fresh flowers. Sometimes they'll toss your child a two-pence. Other than that, the income gap statistic shows, without question, the wrongness of Bloomberg's central assumption in this very issue: That is, a rising tide carries all boats. If the influx of fresh billionaires does what the mayor is suggesting, then the income gap should be tightening, not widening.

Go talk to anyone who has lived in an area with a large wealth concentration. Guess what they'll tell you. Everything costs more—a lot more. In fact, they won't shut up about it, cuz seriously, I get it, the milk was like a million dollars; now can we just sit here and quietly do drugs?

And by the way, what about the "Job Creators" argument (or, as I like to call it, "Trickle-down Economics 2000"). As of the report to which Bloomberg was responding, not only was the income gap widening, not only was the poverty rate rising, but unemployment was also at 8.3%—still about 4% higher than before the recession.

You'd think these magical billionaires radiating their benevolence would be able to fix this, and a new age would dawn upon the land . . . but shockingly, no.

RACE BAITING 101: "HE'S NOT LIKE US!"

So the way it goes is, when a Republican politician is in front of a friendly crowd, he questions the president's legitimacy and patriotism. A surefire winner for riling up the Republican base. It usually goes something like this:

> **"I don't know if Barack Obama was born in the United States or not, but I do know this: in his heart, he's not an American; he's just not an American."**
> —**Rep. Mike Coffman of Colorado, overheard on secret recording made public**

I say Rep. Coffman has a point, think about it: Obama, he's smart, he's well-educated, he's rational . . . he's not like any American I've ever met!

Obama's just trying to fool us into believing he's an American by being born in the United States.

After this statement was discovered ("discovered" because it was posted to YouTube, not by an enemy trying to expose him, but a supporter who thought "more people need to be saying this"), Coffman gets in trouble with regular people in his district and elsewhere.

There is a fascinating video of a reporter confronting Coffman and asking him a series of questions which Coffman gives the exact same answer to. Not the same general answer reworded few different ways; I'm talking the exact same words *verbatim*—like a Stepford Wife.

Here is how it went, and if you can just imagine the congressman with the blankest stare possible coupled with almost robotic chanting, you have this:

Rep. Coffman: *I stand by my statement that I misspoke, and I apologize.*

Reporter: Do you feel the voters are owed a better explanation than "I misspoke?

Rep. Coffman: *I stand by my statement that I misspoke, and I apologize.*

Reporter: Okay, and who are you apologizing to?

Rep. Coffman: *I stand by my statement that I misspoke, and I apologize.*

Reporter: . . . Who is telling you not to talk and to handle it like this?

Rep. Coffman: *I stand by my statement that I misspoke and I apologize.*

Reporter: Is there anything I can ask you that you will answer differently?

Rep. Coffman: *I stand by my statement that I misspoke and I apologize.*

Isn't that just like the liberal media, to expect a conservative to explain why he said something stupid?

Obviously, Coffman is attempting to hypnotize the reporter into leaving him alone. "You will stop asking me that question. You will stop asking me that question. You will stop . . . "

It sounds strange, but this is how Congressman Coffman keeps himself from saying the "N" word.

THE RIGHT WING ALMANAC WITH GARRISON KRISTOL

And here is the Right Wing Almanac for January 10th. It was this week in 1942 that President Franklin Roosevelt signed executive order 9066, which effectively imprisoned every ethnically Japanese person in the U.S. west of the Rockies. It was an action that would remain a horrible black mark on Roosevelt's legacy—having given in to pressure from racists, reactionaries, and land grabbers in the West—even though the move was vehemently opposed by J. Edgar Hoover and even Eleanor Roosevelt herself. It is a day marked every year by Japanese Americans uttering under their breath, "You crippled adulterous asshole."

Speaking of adultery, it was this week in 1999 that the impeachment trial of President William Jefferson Clinton began—Clinton having lied under oath about getting a BJ from an intern. The deposition he was giving at the time was part of an investigation into some land dealings and activities at the White House Travel Office—which strangely kept going further and further afield until they got something really juicy on Clinton. The scandal, although ultimately meaningless, served to freeze the White House legislative agenda for the remainder of Clinton's term. A couple of years later, a sitting vice president would commit treason by outing a CIA operative—and pretty much nothing happened.

And it's the birthday of the greatest whore in public media. Rush Hudson Limbaugh III was born January 12, 1951. Incidentally and ironically, three years later to the day was born Howard Allan Stern—who would give birth to the Shock-Jock genre of broadcasting—and blue-collar guys calling in to CNN to say Baba Booey. Limbaugh, a college drop-out, languished in broadcast obscurity for many years, until 1987, when the FCC repealed the Fairness Doctrine—which required broadcasters not to let some lunatic shoot off their mouth without an adult present to explain why everything he just said was wrong. One year after the repeal, Limbaugh had a national radio show out of WABC in New York. Just to the right of Roy Cohn, Limbaugh has been consistently documented lying on his daily three-hour radio show and said such things as Michael J. Fox is exaggerating his symptoms for sympathy, soldiers who are against the Iraq war are phony soldiers, and Donovan McNabb was only a celebrated quarterback because he is black. He's also a massive hypocrite for, among other things, vilifying the victims of drug and alcohol addiction, while being addicted to OxyContin. Also, he's fat and horrible.

HEY, ASSHOLE!—TODD AKIN

"If it's a legitimate rape, the female body has ways to try to shut that whole thing down."
—Congressman Todd Akin,
not a medical doctor

"Legitimate rape" remark aside, Todd Akin is just a regular, everyday guy who wants to punish victims of rape and incest.

The Representative of Missouri got into big trouble when he said women who'd been legitimately raped don't get pregnant. Akin was trying to make the larger point that we could outlaw abortion and everything would be fine, because even if they get raped, they can't get pregnant cuz nature has a way to "shut that whole thing down."

And that is true; I know it is because I went to the same medical school he did, the one right behind the 7-11.

Of course females can't get pregnant from being raped, and that goes for all females, not just humans, all species of animals. Why, I remember when I was a kid, and I would watch *The Price is Right* with Bob Barker, he would end every show by saying:

"Make sure your pets don't get impregnated, have them spayed, neutered, or raped."*
–Bob Barker, *The Price is Right*

*You don't remember that? Maybe I'm just older than you.

(I remember hearing the "women can't get pregnant if they are raped" theory when I was younger. One time when I was in college, and my wife and I were getting ready to have some wild college-aged sex, and she said, "Jimmy, I don't have any condoms." "Damn, I don't have any money to buy condoms," I replied. "Well, guess you're gonna have to rape me!" she exclaimed.)

Okay, that was fun, but let's get back to Akin.

So he apologized, yet Republican leaders still pressured him to quit running for the Senate. I guess the feeling was, "You just can't say those things about women and rape, no matter how many of us guys personally believe them." Akin explained that he shouldn't have said "legitimate" rape; he meant "forcible" rape as opposed to "consensual" rape, which only exists in Harlequin romance novels. So I've heard.

Unfortunately for the GOP ticket, Akin's remarks only high-lighted Paul Ryan's extreme anti-abortion viewpoint, which logically follows his worship of Ayn Rand. After all, if you let a woman who's been raped get an abortion, you are helping another person, which is wrong.

Overall, this seems to be part of a larger Republican strategy to keep women from voting for them. Even with all this, I still expected Todd Akin to win for two reasons: First, because a majority of voters in Missouri don't know anybody who's been raped. And second, because large numbers of people believe things that are not true . . . for example, that Ronald Reagan was our greatest president, that illegal immigrants are taking away jobs that everybody else wants, or that *Dancing with the Stars* actually features stars.

MESSAGE ON JIMMY'S VOICEMAIL: MICHAEL BLOOMBERG

Jimmy Dore, it's Michael Bloomberg, the billionaire former mayor of New York, New York, the city so nice I bought the mayoral election twice, then paid to have the law changed so I could buy a third term. How filthy rich am I? Well, when I have sex, I ejaculate caviar. That's how rich I am! Holy crap, am I rich!

But I still have a deep concern for minorities, especially an oppressed group that by their very name reveals what a tiny minority they are. I'm speaking of course of the top one percent, the people who earn all the income but get no respect. It seems like everyone is crying over the plight of the Occupy Wall Street rabble, but nobody cares about the men who have been occupying Wall Street for over a century. Do they make a big scene and beg the world for attention? No, they are refined gentlemen who quietly and unobtrusively collect all the wealth and keep it for themselves, without causing a noisy ruckus by stimulating the economy and creating the kind of annoying traffic congestion that happens when the middle class have jobs to go to every day. No, they give those jobs to workers in foreign countries who are happy to get five cents an hour and reside in authoritarian states that would club them to death like baby seals if they so much as raised a peep about income inequality.

That's the kind of thing we need more of here in New York City, Jimmy. This city is a melting pot of many different nationalities, so when I order my police force to crack down on Occupy Wall Street protesters, I'm just paying tribute to the totalitarian regimes that many foreign-born New Yorkers come from. It's just my way of giving them a little piece of home. I can't help it; I'm a sentimentalist. Kind of brings a tear to the eye, doesn't it? Especially when the air is filled with tear gas.

Jimmy, you probably think the top one percent doesn't suffer any deprivations, but they most certainly do. For one thing, they are denied access to foreclosure relief because they can afford to pay their mortgages. And they are completely discriminated against by collection agencies, which never give them so much as a single phone call. In fact, the only time the one percent even get called on the phone is when someone wants to invite them to a weekend in the Hamptons. And Jimmy, I doubt if you know this, but on private Gulf Stream jets, you are now allowed to carry on only two trophy wives, one of which has to be stored underneath the seat in front of you.

So yes, Jimmy Dore, I may be a billionaire, but I still have compassion for an oppressed minority—other billionaires. If I don't look out for them, who will—besides every single person who works in government and law enforcement. Protecting the powerful from the powerless is a big job, so who knows, I may have to buy myself a fourth term as mayor. Frisk you later, Jimmy!

NEWT GINGRICH, CIVIL RIGHTS CHAMPION

"I think race has an enormous impact on decision after decision. You almost have to be blind to America to not realize that we still have very, very deep elements that go all the way back to slavery and segregation. That go all the way back to fundamental differences in neighborhoods and in cultures.

"I think it would be very healthy for the country and the Congress to reevaluate both the criminal justice part up through court, but also to reevaluate the whole way we've dealt with prison and the way in which we've basically created graduate schools for criminality and locking people up in ways that are increasing their inability to function in society."

    —Newt Gingrich, race baiter and horrible person, throwing the dogs off the scent

WTF? This is one of the biggest race baiters alive . . . so this must be a stunt.

First of all, Newt Gingrich needs to never smile again, cuz it is the creepiest dough-boy Barney Rubble shit ever—second only to the moments when he talks sense and has an accurate perspective on an issue.

Clearly, because he is using his intellect to talk sense, it means Gingrich has given up on running for president again.

As with all Gingrich speaking moments, I listened to this just waiting for the other shoe to drop. I kept thinking—sure he's making sense, but that's just so the sting will be all the worse when the turn comes. But remember, this is Gingrich, baby; sometimes he slow-plays the crazy. It's entirely possible he'll just appear on Anderson Cooper's show next week—just his disembodied giant head appearing out of nowhere—and he'll start talking about moon colonies or how the media is behind school shootings.

So this tells me that Newt Gingrich, who for a year and a half publicly referred to the first black president as the "Food Stamp President," actually knows better.

He knew what a horrible thing he was doing when he continually said poor and minority kids lacked a work ethic.

He knew better, and did it anyway.

Imagine that? The race baiter who was asked by Juan Williams if he understood that he was being horribly insulting to blacks, answered "No," he didn't think so, actually did think so and KNEW SO.

It means that Newt Gingrich is craven, empty, mean, and despicable. He clearly knows what he does to try and win elections is denigrating, soulless, and racist . . . and he does it anyway.

It's something I always suspected but could not confirm 100% until he revealed himself. Which is why Anderson Cooper responded to him after his speech with: *"Wow, who are you!?"*

I'm pretty sure after Cooper expressed his surprise, Gingrich said, "Hell yeah man—I'm fucking Gingrich. I'm America's wild card. One minute I'm shamelessly race baiting, next I'm making sense—that's just the crazy party you get when you book the Gingrich. Now if you'd excuse me, I'm gonna go be nice to my wife—BAM!"

UNCIVIL

We've grown accustomed to losing liberty and freedom. Let's face it; we've been living in a semi police state since the advent of the "War on Drugs."

If you're not familiar with this particular war, it's that counter-productive social policy that everybody agrees is a failure, costs $42 billion annually, and is the most destructive thing to our society since polio. It might even be worse than reality TV.

But the people who run the country don't care. Because along with organized crime, local police departments, and the for-profit prison industry, politicians make their living off the war on drugs. Demagoging drug addiction and calling for tougher prison sentences for dealers and users has been the American politicians' bread and butter for decades. It's almost a requirement for elected office, even before the CIA was dumping cocaine in Los Angeles neighborhoods to fund illegal wars in South America.

The point I want to highlight is the drug war was the real start of the end of civil liberties in America. Because who has time to care about civil liberties when there are crackheads in the street and Al Qaeda flies business class? And who has time to worry about this stuff when there's free porn on the Internet?

I do. I grew up in the '80s when fearmongering politicians con-vinced us that *crack* was coming, and it was gonna get us. We didn't really know what it was, but we knew that if we touched it or even looked at it, we would become baby-killing addicts.

The only defense against crack was drug tests for everyone, locking up inner city blacks, and allowing cops to drive tanks on city streets and dress up like combat soldiers. Because how else are you gonna stop a guy from selling pot to his friends unless you invade his home with M-16s at 4am?

We slowly got used to the idea that the government can just take your property and possessions if you were an "exotic gardener." The Constitution applied to everyone except druggies and dealers, (the only dealers I know who should be in prison are the kind who sell used cars).

The fact we allow drug testing is amazing to me. Amazing because they are an incredible invasion of our privacy, and everyone has to take one just to get employed in America. We lose a little more of our privacy and liberty for the sake of pretend safety.

And for those who say that taking a drug test isn't invasive, think of this: would you allow a company to search your closets and drawers in your home looking for drugs as a condition of your employment? Of course not, that would be outrageous. But why are we okay with them going through your penis, vagina, and kidneys looking for drugs? Maybe I'm weird, but the inside of my penis seems a little more personal to me than my sock drawer.

I discovered the perfect solution to end all drug tests. I was recently a guest on a morning radio show, and the station had just been bought by Clear Channel Communications, Inc. I asked the DJ what the biggest difference was working for the old station and now the corporate behemoth Clear Channel.

He said the biggest thing was that they instituted a drug testing policy. I couldn't believe they would drug test employees at a rock & roll radio station! The only occupation intended for freaks, outcasts, and druggies was being intruded on by corporate suits.

I asked the DJ what the result of the new drug testing policy was and I will never forget his answer. He looked up at me with the biggest grin and said, "Everybody failed."

"Everybody failed?" I asked.

"Everybody," he nodded.

"Well, what did they do?" I asked.

"Well they decided . . . that they can't drug test us anymore!"

There's the answer staring us right in the face. All we have to do is make sure everyone takes one toke of weed a month, and we could be rid of this drug testing before next Christmas. They can't fire us all, motherfuckers!!

The point is that the drug war made us okay with giving up some of our rights and really whet the appetites for heavy-handed police tactics.

I won't bore you with the civil liberties lost in the war on terror, but I will tell you about some of them that I have jokes for. First up is an actual quote from President Obama:

"And we want to send the message all around the world to anybody who would do us harm: no act of terror will dim the light of the values that we proudly shine on the rest of the world."

I know that sounds like a hilarious joke that he told at the White House Correspondents' Dinner, but it's not. He was really pretending to believe that stuff.

First of all, it's not true. We changed instantly on 9/11. Not too much . . . just enough to order war crimes, torture, and indefinite detention without trial. Is that a lot?

An act of terror has not only dimmed the light of our values we shine across the world, but it also turned that light of values into a cattle prod and a waterboard. An act of terror turned us into war criminals who start illegal wars, invade countries, torture and murder people, commit war crimes, and steal their resources. We're bullies, which really means we're pussies, and it's why we look the other way with torture and get felt up at the airport.

We got rid of habeas corpus because of 9/11. Stop and think about that for a moment, and then come back and I will explain what habeas corpus means. I looked it up, and it means the government can't just lock you up without charging you with a crime and giving you a trial. This used to happen all the time, which is why somebody had to come up with the famous writ of habeas corpus that says the government can't do that shit.

The writ of habeas corpus is the *linchpin of a free society*, but whatever. We got rid of that when President Obama signed the NDAA act, which repealed the writ of habeas corpus and gave the government the power to detain anyone for however long they want without trial. Kind of the opposite of everything our county is supposed to stand for.

By the way, the writ of habeas corpus is in the Magna Carta. So yeah, we repealed the FUCKING MAGNA CARTA, and we're now operating with a view of liberty from the 1100s, which is too retro for me.

And it's also why, in order to fly on a plane, I have to have my balls patted down and be given an X-ray, which I am sure is perfectly safe. I mean, can there be anything safer than a full-body, government-administered X-ray performed by an airport worker?

I hope there is never another terror attack here in the States, because if that happens, all bets are off. The weaker amongst us will be begging to give up their liberty. I'm pretty sure we are all gonna get tracking bracelets and things will get all *Logan's Run* up in here.

We've become so used to giving up our rights whenever people in power scare the shit out of us that we think harassing citizens based on their skin color is not only okay, but also is a good idea. This is an idea that has spread across the country to police departments from San Diego to New York.

STOP AND FRISK

"The nation's largest police department illegally and systematically singled out large numbers of blacks and Hispanics under its controversial stop-and-frisk policy . . ."
  —Associated Press

"There is just no question that stop, question, frisk has saved countless lives, and most of those lives saved have been black and Hispanic young men."
  —Mayor Bloomberg, former mayor of New York and possibly future presidential candidate

No question it saved their lives? Did it save their lives in the same way slavery helped them save money?

Here is the background info on the NYPD's "Stop and Frisk" Policy.

NY Police stopped and frisked 685,724 people in 2011.

50% of the people who live in NY are black and Latino.

87% of the people stopped and frisked were black or Latino.

90% were innocent of any crime.

That's right, 9 out of 10 of the people stopped and frisked were black or Latino and innocent of any crime.

The NYPD has stopped and frisked 5 million black men; that is more black men than live in New York.

Now, I'm not a math surgeon but . . . isn't that high? I mean, the KKK doesn't put up numbers like that.

So a federal judge took a look, and here's what she found:

"The city's highest officials have turned a blind eye to the evidence that officers are conducting stops in a racially discriminatory manner. . . . The city and its highest officials believe that blacks and Hispanics should be stopped at the same rate as their proportion of the local criminal suspect population. But this reasoning is flawed because the stopped population is overwhelmingly innocent—not criminal."
  —U.S. District Judge Shira Scheindlin

At a news conference, Bloomberg and Police Commissioner Raymond Kelly blasted the ruling, saying the judge ignored historic crime lows and displayed a "disturbing disregard" for the "good intentions" of police officers who do not racially profile.

Oh yeah, the judge ignored historic crime lows almost as badly as the NYPD has ignored the Constitution and the societal effects of racial profiling.

Plus, think about it, the policy was absolutely not racist if you were white.

Bloomberg didn't see how Stop and Frisk broke the law, but he also didn't see how it was breaking the law that he got a third term.

Seriously, it took a judge to figure this out?

The policy might've worked better if the cops had stopped and frisked Wall Street mortgage investment bankers trying to steal people's homes.

The mayor and police tried to argue that it's not a quality of life issue, because everybody in New York who's not rich and white already expects it to suck.

It would be nice if the police chief had to face some tough questions about this from one of our nation's top journalists. But unfortunately, Ray Kelly went on *Meet the Press* instead.

GIVE RACISM A CHANCE

"So they know these guys carry pot and other drugs, and they stop them and frisk and they find them and they send them into the system. That's what drives crime down; get them off the street. The Left hates that, hates it, because it is racial profiling, but it's really criminal profiling. However, there are a number of people who get stopped and frisked who don't have anything, and they get angry, and I understand that.

"But it's a crime-fighting technique that they're now going to take away from the NYPD. And mark my words, street crime will go up because of it."

—Bill O'Reilly, arguing that, if it reduces crime, racism can be a good thing, too.

Hey Bill, there's a pretty low crime rate in China, too. It's surprisingly easy to keep the crime rate low if you don't care about people's basic civil rights or whether they're guilty of a crime.

Sure the cops know who the wise guys and the drug dealers and the muggers are: They're black and Latino and they live in New York City. Bill admits the policy is racist, but he's okay with it because "it works," and because the cops *know who the bad guys are.*

So the cops *KNOW* who the bad guys are, and that's why 9 out of 10 people they stop are completely innocent. And black or Latino.

"However, there are a number of people who get stopped and frisked who don't have anything, and they get angry, and I understand that."

Sure, innocent blacks and Hispanics get angry when they're stopped and frisked, but they need to realize . . . *we're afraid of all of them.*

"But it's a crime-fighting technique that they're now going to take away from the NYPD. And mark my words, street crime will go up because of it."

It's a valuable crime-fighting technique, at least until the police can finally start rounding people up. I wouldn't be surprised if the next thing O'Reilly suggests is a re-education camp in Minnesota.

Seriously NYPD, it's bad enough you get to stop and frisk people without probable cause—but couldn't you violate the fourth amendment without racial profiling?

By the way, Bill, it really doesn't matter that liberals don't like this policy. What actually matters is that citizens of this country are being made to feel like victims of their own society. When it comes to things like this, I am gonna be the first one to say, it doesn't matter what me and my dope-smoking homosexual friends think. Maybe you should ask the poor minorities who get disproportionately singled out for a pat down what they think of this law.

The good news is, these kinds of policies are on their way out in America. The people of New York called for a halt to the Stop and Frisk era of Bloomberg by electing Bill de Blasio. And state by state, marijuana is slowly being legalized, thus depriving police of another excuse to grab ass. The public is coming to the realization that those who have advocated against our basic liberties are truly the "un-American" ones.

THANK GOD FOR RAPE

"I struggled with it myself for a long time, but I came to realize life is that gift from God. And I think even when life begins in that horrible situation of rape, that it is something that God intended to happen."
—Republican Senate nominee Richard Mourdock

Women wouldn't even be an issue if we all gestated our young in fleshy pods the way Scientologists do. However, for the most part, humans are made inside women. It's super gross. Also a miracle, or whatever.

In terms of men's reproductive health, things are fairly simple and straightforward: we're 100% fine 'til about fifty. Then our prostates explode, and then maybe we die, and the great circle of life continues.

On the other hand, women's health as it directly pertains to their reproductive system is super complicated from the get-go. If a woman gets pregnant, then the list of potential problems goes up a ton. In fact, pregnancy in itself is considered a health condition the same way a chronic illness might be.

Now, before I get deeper into this issue, let me say this: There are people in this country who believe that when sperm meets egg, God sends the baby Jesus to magically put a soul in a woman's uterus. If you believe this, you have no business reading this book, and possibly, you have no business reading at all.

Is there an actual war on women? Well, yes and no. No, it is unlikely that right-wing politicos are sitting around a giant map of women trying to figure out how to really screw them. (Note to self—idea for a painting: men standing around a map of a woman.) Rather, the Right comes from a place of utter ignorance, old prejudices, and pre-enlightenment thinking when it comes to policies around women's health. As a matter of political tactics, women's issues are attacked to appease a base (by the way, I suggest you do what I do when imagining the Republican base: Picture a sea of peasants holding torches and pitchforks screaming they must burn the witch). The effect is the same, though: Women's medical rights are attacked as a matter of policy. They are attacked in an organized and systematic way, which could easily be called a war.

The most recent "war on women" became obvious during the debates over the Affordable Care Act. Ya know, Obamacare? The totally socialist program that gives all the money to private health insurance companies? Anywho, you can't talk about health in this country without bringing "lady stuff" into the conversation. So, Right Wing assholes started making noise that they didn't want their tax dollars to pay for women's contraception or abortions. Which, you know, it wouldn't have under this law. Also, which actually happens already when the federal or state government employs a woman—or a dude married to a woman. And even if Obamacare did pay for those things, citizens deciding where tax dollars are spent is probably not a debate we should be having. I, for example, wouldn't want any of my taxes spent on defense. Rather, I'd want to fund really crazy shit, like tiny monkeys riding dogs.

IGNORANCE

The War on Women starts, as so many right-wing efforts do, from ignorance. The perfect example might be Missouri Congressman Todd Akin, (I know we already covered this before but it's too good not to revisit) who, while running for the Senate in 2012, was asked about his views on abortion in the case of rape:

"First of all, from what I understand from doctors, that's really rare. If it's a legitimate rape, the female body has ways to shut that whole thing down."

Yes. Also, you can't get pregnant if you do it standing up in a pool.

Let's start with this: Who are the "doctors" this guy is talking about? Medical doctors? For all of our safety, the AMA should have launched a witch hunt to find these doctors and exterminate them.

Next—legitimate rape. What?! You know, as opposed to pretend rape, where the woman actually wants to get pregnant and have all the rape-attention. To be fair, what the congressman is talking about is the legal difference between rape and statutory rape . . . because people might have been confused that he meant that.

Finally, in case you didn't know, the female body does not have a way of preventing pregnancy. You can tell this because babies are born. See?

This is a UNITED STATES FUCKING CONGRESSMAN! If he's this ignorant, what does that say about the people of Missouri who elected him? It says this: Sex education in the U.S. is terrible. Kids and adults alike are being given half-truths and full lies about a fairly basic biological phenomena. The gaps in the information are being filled by superstition and rumors. Which brings us to our next huge culprit . . .

PRE-ENLIGHTENMENT THINKING

If you teach kids about sex, it encourages them to have it. Man, that is so true. It's not like all mammals want to have sex from the moment they mature. It's not like it is the most basic and powerful biological drive just behind eating, breathing, and shitting. And it's not like teenagers, ignorant of their bodies, get pregnant all the fucking time.

At least a third of sex education in the U.S. is abstinence-only; that is where there is any sex education at all. This approach, at best, omits any reference to contraception and/or disease prevention. At worst, well . . . they just fucking lie.

No kidding, they lie about things like how effective contraception is, HIV transmission rates, the dangers of abortion, and if the bee calls the bird afterwards. This approach to sex education is condemned by The American Psychological Association, the American Medical Association, the National Association of School Psychologists, the American Academy of Pediatrics, the American Public Health Association, the Society for Adolescent Medicine, and the American College Health Association. Oh, and did I mention that the federal government gives lots of grants to fund this type of sex education?

Yes, nothing prevents abortion like not using birth control.

Look, if we're gonna teach kids this way, I say we go all the way and tell them things like, "You can cure warts by rubbing a potato on them in the light of a full moon."

PREJUDICE

So, for a minute or two in 2012, former Senator Rick Santorum was considered a serious candidate for the presidency . . . of the United States . . . for real. Rick Santorum is an ultra-conservative Catholic who would outlaw the female orgasm if given the chance. Santorum's Super-Pac was heavily funded by billionaire businessman Foster Friess. When asked about Santorum's positions, Mr. Friess dropped this little gem:

"You know, back in my days, they used Bayer aspirin for contraception. The gals put it between their knees, and it wasn't that costly."

Now, as a professional comedian, I gotta say: Know your room. That one might have been your closer at the Secret Evil White Guy Club, but it's not gonna play in other venues. Workshop it a little, man.

There are still lots of these old white misogynists running the debate in this country. They think women are obligated to keep their virginity 'til marriage, or they are sluts if they don't. Let me give you another example: In 2012, the House of Representatives held hearings on contraceptives in healthcare—hearings overseen entirely by male congressmen that included deposing people like priests . . . and other priests. So, a Georgetown University law student, Sandra Fluke, was asked to testify . . . then told not to testify by the Republican-controlled committee. Eventually, Ms. Fluke got to speak at the Democratic Steering Committee. She gave a compelling and truthful argument why even religious institutions like Georgetown University should provide contraception benefits. Then, in response to this, Rush Limbaugh (an old friend of mine), said this:

> **"[Fluke] essentially says that she must be paid to have sex—what does that make her? It makes her a slut, right? It makes her a prostitute. She wants to be paid to have sex. She's having so much sex she can't afford the contraception. She wants you and me and the taxpayers to pay her to have sex."**

This from the guy who used his prescription benefits to buy Oxy-Contin.

We should also mention that most health insurance covers Viagra.

THE WAR

The War on Women comes from the dark corners of stupidity, and it is waged by perpetuating the dark corners. Remember, all of the statements quoted herein are from the last few years—all made in the furtherance of the Right's agenda. I'll let crazy lady Michele Bachmann have the floor on this one:

> **"I will tell you that I had a mother last night come up to me here in Tampa, Florida, after the debate. She told me that her little daughter took that vaccine, that injection, and she suffered from mental retardation thereafter."**
> **–Rep. Michele Bachmann (R-MN), on the HPV vaccine, Fox News interview, Sept. 12, 2011**

Granted, that's an extreme example—but it's just so awesome. To this day, no one really knows what UNITED STATES CONGRESSWOMAN Bachmann was talking about. The HPV vaccine doesn't even make you bored. And the lady who told her about the HPV-retarded daughter has never been found. Maybe she was a ghost.

The HPV vaccine helps prevent cervical cancer, for God's sake. How can you be against that? Well, if you're Michele Bachmann—or any right-wing nut job—you think an HPV vaccine encourages young women to fornicate with wart-laden men. How do you stop this? By telling a giant lie about the HPV vaccine. Don't want women to have abortions because it makes Jesus cry? Tell total lies about the dangers of abortion or the consciousness of a fetus. I just think you could come up with better lies. For example, did you know that sometimes an abortion goes horribly awry and makes more babies?

So far, we've been talking about contraception and abortion—things which give a woman and her doctor some control over reproductive health and related issues. It's serious stuff. In addition to women's health, their financial, social, and psychological well-being are at stake. Unwanted pregnancies have serious consequences for society as a whole. These matters alone would be sufficient stuff for a war on women. However, let me give you one more example—actual war:

The United States used to do business with military contractors that barred female employees from suing for on-the-job rape cases. No kidding. Minnesota Senator Al Franken introduced a law that would stop this practice. And you'd assume a law like that would be a no-brainer, right? Wrong. Although the Senate passed the bill, *thirty* senators voted against it—voted against a bill that says, "Hey, you got raped; maybe you should have the right to sue someone or something . . . "

Since the wars in Afghanistan and Iraq began, the problem of rape in the military has grown horrifically. A woman in the military is *much* more likely to be raped by a fellow serviceman than killed in combat. It took until this year for Congress to pass any laws on the matter—and it's a pretty fucking weak law. And they roundly rejected allowing a rape victim to go outside their chain of command in order to seek justice.

In 2013, 22 senators and 138 congressmen voted against reauthorizing the Violence Against Women Act. Pro-life groups have openly conspired with the American Legal Exchange Council (ALEC) to pass abortion restriction laws in every state. In 2011 alone, 92 state laws were passed which restricted women's access to reproductive services.

SECRET POLLS AND OTHER RIGHT WING ALTERNATIVE REALITIES

"Today we will talk about the real poll numbers; the media is circulating this myth that Romney is in serious trouble. Well on Friday, I looked at the real poll numbers by an organization I can't name, but I trust it."
—Dick Morris

Have you ever heard of a "Secret Poll?" That's both the craziest and most ominous thing I've ever heard. It's like his source is a heroine dealer who does illegal polling on the side.

FYI: When someone says, "Trust what I'm saying because I have a secret source," it never works out well. That ends in the bombing of Cambodia, the invasion of Iraq, and me thinking my girlfriend won't get pregnant cuz we did it in a jacuzzi.

HOLY FREAK OUT, BATMAN

"Do you know the name of the villain in this [new Batman] movie? BANE. . . . What is the name of the venture capital firm that Romney ran . . . ? BAIN! . . . Do you think that it is acci-dental that the name of the really vicious . . . villain in this movie is named 'BANE'?"
—Rush Limbaugh

If Rush Limbaugh wasn't a thing, and you did a sketch where you repeated things he says verbatim, you would be considered a comic genius.

And most people do instinctively think Limbaugh is funny—until the moment they realize there are millions of registered voters who totally believe this stuff. I mean, it's still funny, just not in a ha-ha kind of way, more in a Russian tragedy sort of way.

It must be so liberating not having to edit your thoughts based on logic or any sort of moral compass. It's like dream poetry or something. OxyContin must really open up your consciousness.

If you watch Rush Limbaugh broadcasting, he says this stuff while referring to notes on his desk. That means he had to write down a flow chart or something to remember this strained logic based on an ad hominem. In my day, when someone went on an insane rant, they didn't bring notes; they took the time to rehearse. It's called craftsmanship, you fat fuck.

TEA BAGGING RELIEF

 "If when a family is struck with tragedy—like the family of Joplin . . . let's say they had $10,000 set a aside to do something else with, to buy a new car, and then they were struck with a sick member of the family or something, and needed to take that money and apply it to that, that's what they would do, because families don't have unlimited money. And, really, neither does the federal government."
—Eric Cantor, explaining why he won't fund relief for people wiped out by a tornado in Joplin, Missouri

You know how everyone in Congress is in the pocket of the health insurance and pharmaceutical industries? And that's why you get screwed and go bankrupt when someone in your family gets sick? Well *now* . . . we're doing that with tornados, too. You can have your tornado relief if you want it . . . *but*, you're going to have the ride the bus from now on, and no healthcare when you retire. That's what America is about—choice! (i.e., funneling money upward).

In Eric Cantor's world, the problem with those people in Joplin is that they were just going along not saving their money and were totally unprepared to be wiped out by a tornado. Why should the rest of us suffer? We've got to stop wasting federal money on people whose lives were destroyed by tornados and who now have no homes. If we're going to spend money, let's spend it on people who already have somewhere to live.

While it seems like a blunder, this is a brilliant political strategy designed to shore up the heartless-prick vote, whose ideology seems to be:

"I'm a Republican, and we believe in personal responsibility, not government handouts. So when I say that 'our hearts go out to the victims of Sandy,' we mean that's all that goes out to them, got it? Not aid or government resources, just stuff that doesn't cost money."

BENGHAZI, DONE THAT

In the realm of presidential scandals manufactured by the right wing, the "Obama didn't call the Benghazi 'act of terror' an 'act of terror'" was one of the weakest. Maybe it was because there was actual video tape of Obama making an official statement from the White House calling it an "act of terror"? Hard to tell.

So this is where the right-wing alternative reality bubble can get you into trouble. They repeated the "Obama didn't call the Benghazi attack a 'terrorist attack'" line so often and with such confidence that they started to believe it themselves, including their presidential nominee.

That's not the real problem though; the real trouble comes when the nominee repeats this completely manufactured fact in front of a newsperson who accidentally does their job and debunks a falsehood presented on national television.

Mitt Romney: "It took the president 14 days to call the Benghazi attack an 'act of terror.'"

Candy Crowley: "He did, in fact sir, call it an act of terror."

(crowd applause)

It was a huge tactical mistake by Romney, brought on by spending too much time in the Right-Wing Alternate Reality Bubble, where actual facts are optional.

Here is how that moment was interpreted by Rush Limbaugh:

"In a real world, she would've committed career suicide last night; she committed an act of journalistic terror or malpractice last night; if there were any journalistic standards, what she did last night would've been the equivalent of blowing up her career like a suicide bomber, but there aren't any journalistic standards anymore."
—Rush Limbaugh, champion of journalism

Hey Rush, if there were any journalistic standards, you would've been waterboarded years ago. If there were any journalistic standards, we wouldn't have spent a trillion dollars in Iraq and still be in the longest war in our nation's history. If there were any journalistic standards, we would've been warned about the impending banking meltdown. If there were any journalistic standards, the whole fucking country might turn upside-down.

Now a lot of people would say that fact-checking politicians in real time is exactly what has been missing from our political discourse, and they would praise Candy Crowley. But then there are those who are allergic to facts and accurate information, like our friend Tucker Carlson, who, by the way, has dropped the bow tie and changed his image from *"that douche in a bow tie"* to *"that douche in a regular tie."*

> **"She threw the president a lifeline . . . they should just eliminate moderators overall."**
> —Tucker Carlson, loser

Yeah, if we could only get rid of the moderators and refs and journalists and reporters, and nobody would ever fact check anything; then we could get some shit done.

That is the right wing wet dream: a world without fact checkers or investigative reporters that actually investigate. Tucker Carlson accusing other people of being attention seekers from the headquarters of Fox News is like . . . you write the joke, America, this is a gimme.

Here, just think of someone condemning something they themselves are doing at that very moment. Make it something really ridiculous—usually sexual. OK, now using a confident and funny voice in your head, compare Tucker Carlson to that. Now enjoy that joke you just made for the rest of the day.

The lifeline thrown was for Romney, who was attempting to shame the president of the United States—and before he could keep digging that hole, she corrected him. That is a favor, man. She just did for him what my wife has to do for me at cocktail parties all the time. It's a thankless, depressing, co-dependent job. Candy Crowley doesn't deserve Fox's derision; she deserves a twelve-step program.

And here is why they want to get rid of fact checkers: The next day, after Candy Crowley poked a hole in the Right Wing Bubble, John Sununu, our favorite "nerd-bully," went on Soledad O'Brien's show on CNN and tried to peddle the debunked claim again, except this time yelling it at the top of his lungs.

Sununu: All the apologists for this White House . . . have been lying about the president trying to deceive America, that that tragedy was the result of a video rather than acknowledge right from the beginning that this was a well-planned, well-executed terrorist attack.

O'Brien: You realize what he said during the debate was, "The day after the attack here was the statement from the Rose Garden and said 'no acts of terror will ever shake the resolve'. . ."

Then she gets cut off reading from the transcript by Sununu.

Sununu: He got caught lying . . . if you are going to dwell on this YOU'RE OUT OF YOUR MIND!!

A classic nerd-bully technique: When lying doesn't work—start lying *louder.*

Of course, to lay it on thick and with less brain cells, we have *Fox and Friends.* You know how *Fox and Friends* is supposed to feel like it's just three normal people getting together to chat about current events over coffee? I've watched quite a bit of this show, and I gotta say, most restaurant scenes from *Sex and the City* feel closer to a real political discussion.

"The problem was Candy Crowley as the moderator . . . it was like she was the ref, she threw a flag; you're not supposed to do that. The time for fact checking is after an event, not during it."
—Steve Ducey

Yup, the time for fact checking is after the event. That's how the

New York Times does it. They just publish whatever they think, then correct it in retractions later. It's called journalism, asshole.

Honestly, it's like *Limbaugh for Dummies*, except the dummies are the hosts. So it's more like *Dummies for Dummies*.

And then after Candy Crowley pointed out that President Obama did call Benghazi an "act of terror," Megyn Blonde Lady at Fox News says this: (Please sit down for this one and make sure you're not drinking liquid that could fly out your nose.)

"Declaring something an 'act of terror' is not necessarily the same thing as declaring it a 'terrorist attack.'"
—Megyn Blonde Lady, Fox News

When you call terrorism an "act of terror," the terrorists win.

PHONE CALL WITH GEORGE W. BUSH

JIMMY: We'll be celebrating another anniversary of September 11th soon, and I'm fortunate to be on the phone with the man who protected us immediately following that attack . . . former President George W. Bush. Mr. President, thank you for being on the show.

BUSH: Jimmy, it's nice to be on the phone with you. I listen to it all the time.

JIMMY: You listen to my show?

BUSH: No, I listen to my phone. (chuckles) That was a joke, JD.

JIMMY: Mr. President, I wanted to ask you about Syria.

BUSH: Ask me anything. I know all about Syria.

JIMMY: I'm sure you do, Mr. President.

BUSH: It's the one that's not Libya. (chuckles) Jimmy, I'm just pretending I'm too dumb to know the difference between Libya and . . . the other one. I actually do know the difference.

JIMMY: I'm sure you do, Mr. President. You had that whole Situation Room with all the maps in it. Do you think Presi-dent Obama has botched Syria?

BUSH: I think "botched" is a strong word.

JIMMY: I don't think it is, Mr. President.

BUSH: Okay, maybe it's not. To each his own. See how you're not roping me in? I'm doing pretty good so far.

JIMMY: Do you think Obama fumbled his Syria policy and was only bailed out because John Kerry ad-libbed that remark about Syria giving up its chemical weapons?

BUSH: I can't comment on John Kerry because I don't know the man.

JIMMY: You ran against Kerry for re-election in 2004.

BUSH: Was that him? I think he's had some work done. Is it just me?

JIMMY: Mr. President, it's difficult to talk with you when you refuse to even parrot conservative talking points. Let me help you out . . . you're a Republican, Obama's a Democrat, doesn't that mean he's weak and wishy-washy in dealing with our enemies?

BUSH: I see what you're trying to do, Jimmy. You're reading my mind and saying it out loud on the radio. Or is this the Twitter?

JIMMY: Mr. President, do you think Obama painted himself into a corner over this whole question of Assad allegedly using chemical weapons?

BUSH: I was president, Jimmy; I know what that's like, when you're in a corner and you're painting yourself . . . recently I painted myself taking a shower.

JIMMY: Do you think the United States should bomb Syria?

BUSH: Jimmy, I'm a private citizen now . . . with a huge pension I don't need, and Secret Service protection for the rest of my life, which I may still need. No matter what you try to do as president, it comes out extremely terrible. That wasn't just me.

JIMMY: Doesn't it seem to you that Obama trapped himself into announcing an attack on Syria, then asked for Congress' permission just to buy some time?

BUSH: I can't really say, Jimmy but yeah, that was pretty damn stupid.

JIMMY: Okay! Finally!

BUSH: I don't know what he was thinking there, Jimmy. The president has the right to start a limited war under certain constitutional guidelines.

JIMMY: And what constitutional guidelines are those, Mr. President?

BUSH: Whatever constitutional guidelines he needs to start a war. I mean every war is different. My wars were different from this war. It's like apples and . . . war.

JIMMY: Do you think we'll have a massive conflagration in the Middle East if we attack Syria?

BUSH: Sometimes you have to go to war, Jimmy. I didn't want to invade Iraq, but I had no choice.

JIMMY: Can't you just admit that Iraq was a gigantic, tragic mistake?

BUSH: We won't know for sure, Jimmy, until you're dead.

JIMMY: Until I'm dead?

BUSH: You, me . . . Kirk Douglas, Mickey Rooney. Then once we're dead, we still won't know. Which is why I've been painting.

JIMMY: Mr. President, as a liberal, I have to say I'm disappointed in Obama.

BUSH: I can understand that, Jimmy. You had such high hopes for him. He sure didn't live up to that poster.

JIMMY: No, he didn't. Obama's done every illegal thing you did, and in some ways he's been even worse.

BUSH: I see the glass as half full, Jimmy. He's like my fourth term, if I were a little more articulate and much more black.

JIMMY: Mr. President, what the hell's wrong with our government when each and every president, Democrat and Republican, gets roped into these unwinnable wars and endless catastrophes? When are we as a nation going to be honest that everything we do is about oil and making deals with the worst dictators on earth? Where is this leading us, Mr. President? How do we survive as a civilization?

BUSH: You know, Obama's right about one thing, Jimmy . . . you're a hothead.

JIMMY: Thank you for speaking with us, Mr. President.

BUSH: I enjoyed it, JD.

JIMMY: Did you really?

BUSH: (chuckles) No.

HEY, ASSHOLE!–MARK LEVIN

"I want to make a statement to the Republican Party, to the president, and to the media. Conservatives, we do not accept bi-partisanship in the pursuit of tyranny, period.

"We will not negotiate the terms of economic and political servitude, period. We will not abandon our children to a dark and bleak future. We will not accept a fate that is alien to the legacy we inherited from every single future generation in this country. We will not accept social engineering by politicians and bureaucrats who treat us like lab rats rather than self-sufficient, independent human beings.

"There are those in this country who choose tyranny over liberty; they do not speak for us. Fifty-seven million of dictate to us under our constitution. We are the alternative; we will resist. We are not going to surrender to this. We

will not be passive; we will not be compliant in our own demise. We're not good losers; you better believe we're sore losers. A good loser is a loser forever!"
—Mark Levin, talk show host, the day after the
2012 presidential election, not handling it well

If you've never before heard the definition of a histrionic personality disorder . . . well, you have now.

This seems like a good statement to roll out the next time Republicans start talking about who's a patriot.

I'd like to note, this guy has a nationally syndicated radio show. When I was a kid, before the death of the Fairness Doctrine, this dope would've had a pirate radio show out of his mom's garage that reached maybe three blocks. And though I am a huge free speech advocate, I'd like to note that the FCC has no opinion about the inflammatory rhetoric of this lunatic, but they are still obsessed with Janet Jackson's tit.

I like the fact that the premise of his whole rant is that he and all conservatives are somehow oppressed victims . . . you know, like black people in the Jim Crow South. Try to imagine what this guy is like when the gas company guy comes to read the meter: "Why don't you just put shackles on me now, big powerful gas man!"

One thing that sticks out is that he calls himself a "self-sufficient, independent human being." I'll grant you, paternalism is a topic worthy of discussion; however, this guy just sounds like a child declaring he's a "big boy." A grown man in the middle of a tantrum doesn't exactly sound mature, so much as someone who might want to give himself over to the care of the state (in the form of a local mental hospital).

This guy is like the Black Panther leader of people who don't want to pay a one-cent tax on soda.

NEWS FLASH! PRESIDENT RELEASES LONG-FORM BIRTH CERTIFICATE

"I'm very proud of myself because I've been able to accomplish something that nobody else has been able to accomplish; I am really honored to have played such a big role in hopefully getting rid of this issue."
—Donald Trump on President Obama releasing his long- form birth certificate

OK, LOOK—my head is about to explode because a game show host just made the president dance for him. FUCKING DONALD TRUMP isn't even RUNNING FOR PRESIDENT but news people can't help but stick a mic in his face and TAKE HIM SERIOUSLY! In a few short news cycles, these people have turned us into a joke country! I feel like Canada could come down here and pants us at any moment, and we'd have to take it.

Even after the president released his long-form birth certificate, most Birthers and Teabaggers still find him suspiciously black.

WHAT'S
WRONG
WITH
DEMOCRATS?

MESSAGE ON JIMMY'S VOICEMAIL:

PRESIDENT BARACK OBAMA, 4:50pm

"Jimmy Dore, it's Barack Obama. Did you see my speech about taxing the rich the other day? Pretty inspiring, huh? Yup, I'm telling you, I've had it with these fat cat millionaires and billionaires, and I am going to throw the bums out the minute I'm elected to office! That's right, on my first day in the White House, I am going to make some changes that are really going to . . .

What's that? . . . Excuse me, Jimmy, one of my aides is on the line. . . .

Say it again . . .

Really?

Wow, you don't say.

Say, Jimmy, do you like trivia? Well, here's a tidbit I'm not sure you knew about: Apparently, I've been the president of the United States for the past six years! Wow, who knew? I guess that's why there's always a 21-gun salute wherever I go. I assumed that guns were being drawn on me because

I'm a black man, but actually, I'm the leader of the free world!

I guess maybe the reason I always feel so powerless despite my lofty title is that I spend so much time hanging around bankers and Wall Street tycoons. These are some fancy people. They eat elegant meals and sip imported champagne, but I'm just a regular guy with simple tastes, so all I do is drink their Kool-Aid. This drink is like a potion that has a kind of Dr. Waffle and Mr. Hype effect on me. In the oval office, I'm Dr. Waffle—always waffling and caving and giving in on what are supposed to be my core beliefs. On the podium stump, I'm Mr. Hype—always pushing progressive ideals with dazzling oratorical skills that get crowds all hyped up and excited until I return to Washington and then disappoint everyone with my waffling again. Jimmy, I know the country is in a depression, but from my base I've been doing everything I can to make it a bipolar depression.

Jimmy, my entire presidency has been based on the idea of hope, and that is still true. I hoped my Republican opponents sucked so bad you'd just have to vote for me . . . and it came true. I was going to change my campaign slogan, "Change We Can Believe In," to "Caves We Can Believe In," but I've finally settled on a new slogan: "Barack Obama: You're Going To Vote For Him Anyway, So Just Shut Up."

Well, Jimmy, it's been almost five minutes since I compromised on something, so I'd better get going. Wait a minute. Why is there a private jet fueled up and waiting for me? . . . Oh, right, I forgot. I'm the friggin' president! I should put a string on my finger to remind me. Thanks, Jimmy, see you later!"

THE AUDACITY OF COMPROMISE

"What folks are looking for is some compromise up here, that's what folks want; they understand they are not going to get 100% of what they want."

—Pres. Obama lying about people wanting him to cut Medicare and Social Security

Right, people are not going to get a hundred percent of what they want, especially if they wanted Obama not to cave in on Social Security. I think this is Obama's way of preventing Republicans from screwing our most vulnerable citizens—by doing it himself.

Oh yeah, Barack, that's what they were saying when they voted for you, they were all saying PLEASE COMPROMISE and cut my Medicare and Social Security to help finance two wars, tax cuts for millionaires, and massive bank bailouts.

The specific change to Social Security that President Obama is proposing is something called Chained CPI, which stands for "Chained Consumer Price Index for All Urban Consumers." In short, it's a way to tie Social Security benefits to the rate of inflation, or the rise in prices over time.

What's important to know is that chained CPI would mean Social Security benefits would increase at a slower rate than they do using the current index.

This is called a "cut in Social Security," something the Republicans usually propose and the Democrats usually fight against. So it was pretty awkward for Nancy Pelosi when a reporter asked her:

"Do you consider that a cut in Social Security?"
—Reporter asking Nancy Pelosi about Obama's proposal to switch Social Security to a "Chained CPI," which

reduces the amount of money people receive from
Social Security.

"No, I consider it a strengthening of Social Security."
—Nancy Pelosi, apparently answering that question
on "opposite day"

See, this strengthens Social Security by keeping billions of dollars
out of the hands of elderly spendthrifts. And remember it's not a benefit
cut; a benefit cut is when you cut benefits. This is more like a *reduction
in how much money people get*. Two different things.

But what's important is that the Democrats showed they can be
flexible by giving away something they swore up and down they
wouldn't.

MODERATES

Unlike most people, I hate moderates. I say, pick a side. I think if you
are a Democrat, be one, if you are a Republican, be that, but please
don't pretend to be both. Nothing great was achieved by moderates.
Its called the Declaration of Independence, not the "Declaration of
Getting Along."

I know most people like the idea of moderates because they operate under the assumption that the best ideas lie somewhere in the
middle, and moderates seem to imply that they are more reasonable.
I say, what is reasonable about voting for the Iraq war? What is reasonable about shifting the tax burden to the middle class and working
poor while deregulating Wall Street? And while we're at it, what
exactly is the moderate position on torture? Are they for a moderate
amount of torture?

I could go on and on, and will in the following section, where I
highlight the problems facing Democrats.

EVAN BYE BYE

> "If the president says . . . look I'm willing to have 2 or 3 to 1
> spending reductions vs. tax increasings, and I'm willing to
> have a pro-growth tax reform package, you can really get
> something done here."
> —Evan Bayh, Corporate Tool, Shitty Democrat

Yeah, see, since the president won the election . . . what we will do is cut 3 dollars in spending for every 1 dollar in tax revenue. Why that plan? See, the way it works is this: When the Republicans win an election, you implement the Republican plan, and when the Democrats win an election . . . you implement the Republican plan. That's called "being a moderate."

MODERATE: ED RENDELL

> "The people want us to get together and do something . . .
> we need more Republicans who are going to stand in there
> and say, 'Yes, spending is the issue'. . . . We've got to have
> legitimate entitlement reform, and our side, we've got to
> do this.
> "I was on *The Cycle*, one of MSNBC's shows, and I suggest-
> ing raising the age of Medicare; given the fact that we are
> living longer, isn't necessarily a bad idea. The three pro-
> gressives hosts . . . you would've thought I proposed trea-
> son to the American government."
> —Ed Rendell, former Pennsylvania governor,
>   super shitty Democrat

Oh fuck, I knew that Rendell had turned into a corporate cocksucker, but this is a little ridiculous.

That was Ed's opening salvo to start a back-slapping session of a panel full of self-proclaimed "moderates" on MSNBC.

The show was hosted by Michael Smerconish and featured Republican moderate Steve LaTourette of Ohio along with Rendell. Smerconish is a right-wing talk show host who often fills in for Bill O'Reilly, so of course Chris Matthews has him guest host his show, too, just in case anybody got the crazy idea that there was a difference between Fox and MSNBC, I guess.

Let me be super clear about something: Ed Rendell is a Democrat—a major player in the Democratic party—and after reading that quote from him, it's easy to understand why the Democrats have trouble finding their car keys in their asses.

Let's break down his statement, shall we?

"The people want us to get together and do something—"

Fair enough. I, as one of the people, will affirm that I would like the people to whom I pay taxes to do shit actually do some shit.

"... we need Republicans; we need more Republicans who are gonna stand in there and say, 'Yes, spending is the issue.'"

Right and—wait, what? That doesn't even make sense—I mean, that's all those guys ever fucking say. And more of them saying it? Well that would be like having extra screaming cats—when really, just one is plenty.

Wait, is Ed Rendell one of those Democrats that's—what do you call it?—oh yeah, a Republican?

"And we've gotta have legitimate entitlement reform. And on our side Mike, we've gotta do this . . . I suggested raising the age of Medicare, given the fact that we're living longer, isn't a necessarily bad idea. The three progressive hosts? You would have thought I proposed treason . . ."

I'm guessing they didn't react as if it was treason he was suggesting so much as it was kicking elderly people in the genitals. Because the health insurance industry isn't real wild about covering old, sick people; they consider being forty a pre-existing condition, so—over sixty-five is gonna be a problem.

And I don't know if Ed Rendell has noticed this, but outside of professional politics, we live in a pretty age-ist and competitive society. Most industries want their old people to retire—and most young people looking for work want old people to retire—oh, and guess what? A lot of people who have been working for forty-some odd years want to retire.

Always be careful when people use the word reform, cuz a lot of the time when they say "reform," what they really mean is "fucking." Remember welfare reform? Sounds like it was a way to make welfare more efficient and really deal with the issue of poverty in this country . . . turned out, not so much.

Here's a term I've never heard: "Pentagon reform."

And not to keep kicking a dead horse, but Ed Rendell just can't keep cheerleading for members of the party he's not in to take control of government.

"—and even if it means there are a few more Republicans in Senate and the Congress, if they're reasonable Republicans who are moderates conservatives, that's a good prescription for America—"

Little known fact about Ed Rendell; he hasn't read a newspaper or watched a TV since 1987. This is why he thinks there are still enough moderate Republicans out there to do things, when in fact, you couldn't put together enough moderate Republicans for a game of laser tag. When a Democrat says the only people who can fix our problems are Republicans, isn't it time to turn in your Democratic Party membership card? We need to give MITCH McCONNELL MORE POWER?

BTW, working people aren't living longer; rich people are. Yes, rich people are living longer, you know, people who don't work for a living. Why does no one ever point that out?

So, here's the other politician on the "moderate" panel: outgoing Republican congressman from Ohio, Steve LaTourette. And, to be fair, he's likely one of the last truly moderate Republicans left—which must be a special kind of internal torment to suffer.

> **"Well, my next endeavor, the non-paying one, is going to be to head up the Republican Main Street Partnership, to give comfort and cover to both center-right Republicans and center-left (I guess) Democrats, to stand up to the fringe groups on the right and left, who have the courage to do the right thing . . .**
>
> **"You know if Governor Rendell and I were in charge, we would have fixed this thing in about a week and a half, and everybody knows what the solutions are . . ."**
> **—Republican Steve LaTourette**

So let's take a moment and unpack what that means, exactly. First of all, that's a curious choice of words, isn't it? "Comfort and cover"—very much like "aiding and abetting."

"—to stand up to the fringe groups on the right and left, who have the courage to do the right thing . . ."

Yes, those fringe groups are exactly the same. You know, on the left, the people who want to preserve Medicare, Medicaid, and Social Security, because they have been and remain effective and humane programs that address massive social problems.

And then on the right, the people who don't think we should pay taxes or have laws and think human greed will fix everything. Yes, those are exactly the same in how fringe-y they are.

Has anyone else noticed that Republicans have lately adopted the word "courage" to mean "willingness to fuck the poor?" You never hear the term courage when someone risks their political career to, say, stand up to Grover Norquist or tell the NRA to go fuck themselves . . . Oh, you know why? . . . because that never happens.

"You know if Governor Rendell and I were in charge, we would have fixed this thing in about a week and a half . . ."
—Republican Steve LaTourette

Yeah, those two could solve all our problems in a week and a half, but how? Let me guess: cut Social Security and Medicare, deregulate Wall Street, and start another war . . . am I warm?

I'm guessing at the end of that week and a half, my parents would be living with me, and the capital gains tax would be exactly the same.

"And everybody knows what the solutions are—"

Correction: Everyone knows what the easy solutions are. Fuck the old and poor, cuz what are they gonna do about it?

DICK DURBIN—SHITTY DEMOCRAT

"In 2037, Social Security as we know it will fall off a cliff. There's a 22% reduction in payments, which is really not something we can tolerate; if we deal with it today, it's an easier solution than waiting."
—Sen. Dick Durbin, bad Democrat

Yeah, I guess since Senator Dick Durbin has fixed all the problems in the country that will happen while he is alive, so now he is gonna start working on the problems that will come up after he is dead. How thoughtful of him.

Senator Durbin is currently the Democratic majority whip. That's an official position in the Senate? Do you think these guys know about the whole slavery thing—like that we used to actually whip other human beings and all that, and maybe that title might evoke a history we might not want to evoke? OK.

And what he's talking about is Social Security, and how its solvency runs out in 27 years, and then it will only be able to pay out 70% of benefits. And what he's saying is, we should fix that. I totally agree; I think we should fix Social Security, only I think we should do it right after we fix literally every other public policy issue ever.

Because, you know, the polar ice caps are melting, we're still in Afghanistan, and healthcare is one-fifth of the goddamn economy. That's just off the top of my head. I'm pretty sure given time, I could come up with a couple dozen other things which will happen in the next ten years—let alone the next 26 years.

You gotta wonder what Senator Durbin's daily to-do list looks like. I bet number one is, "Get tickets and book hotel for 2024

Olympics; make plans for my 90th birthday party in 2031," and forty items down the list is, "Eat food so you don't die today."

DRONING ON AND ON

"The White House says the death of Al Qaeda's second-in-command is a major blow to the terror network; Pakistani security forces say that Abu-Yaya-Alibi died in a U.S. drone strike; he was mistakenly reported killed back in 2009."
—MSNBC news

Did you catch that? That guy we said we killed before—but didn't? Well, it turns out, we just killed him now . . . *for reals*! How do we know? The government told us. You know, the guys who told us they killed him before, but didn't? Those guys told us.

Those same guys told us that all this killing without a trial was constitutional (when it's not), and that it would end terrorism (when it doesn't). And then it is MSNBC's job to pass along that information without a critical eye. Looking at information the government gives us about an illegal government killing spree is the job of anti-American traitors, not journalists.

I don't get how we are getting away with the drone strikes in other countries. Isn't attacking people in other countries an act of war? Aren't drone strikes illegal and unconstitutional? And aren't they causing more problems than they solve? Doesn't killing Al Qaeda with drones that also kill lots of innocents only create more people who want to kill Americans?

Having a kill list is gross, too; we should have a "most wanted" list, but not a "kill without trial" list. I thought this kind of thing was a war crime?

Well, that's tricky. If you base your answer on international law or the U.S. Constitution then yeah, it's super illegal.

But if you base your decision on the word of the government (you know, the people doing the drone killing), then no, it's super legal and the Christian thing to do.

Except those American-hating-hippies at the ACLU don't agree with the government and have decided to sue over it, stating on their website:

> **"The executive branch has, in effect, claimed the unchecked authority to put the names of citizens and others on 'kill lists' on the basis of a secret determination, based on secret evidence, that a person meets a secret definition of the enemy.**
>
> **"The targeted killing program operates with virtually no oversight outside the executive branch, and essential details about the program remain secret, including what criteria are used to put people on CIA and military kill lists or how much evidence is required."**

OK let's review:

President places name of American citizen to be killed on "kill list" based on decision made in *secret*, using *secret* information gathered in *secret*, and carrying out the killing in *secret*, while keeping all information about the entire program *secret*.

OK, what's the problem? State killing done in total secret with no oversight or accountability? How is that out of step with an open society committed to transparency in a government dedicated to freedom, liberty, and civil rights? It's a real head scratcher.

But is it really illegal? Does it really violate international law and the U.S. Constitution?

Let's let the ACLU explain:

"Outside of armed conflict zones, the use of lethal force is strictly limited by international law and, when it comes to U.S. citizens, the Constitution. Specifically, lethal force can be used only as a last resort against an imminent threat to life.

"Even in the context of an armed conflict against an armed group, the government may use lethal force only against individuals who are directly participating in hostilities against the U.S. Regardless of the context, whenever the government uses lethal force, it must take all possible steps to avoid harming civilian bystanders. These are not the standards that the executive branch is using."

OK, so the United States uses drones to kill anyone at anytime, anywhere if the secret information collected in secret says you are a secret enemy of the United States.

Feel safer?

FREEDOM OF THE PRESS . . .
FOR THE PROPER PEOPLE

"Thanks to important bipartisan compromises, we've put together a strong bill that balances the need for national security with that of a free press."
—Sen. Chuck Schumer, rationing the First Amendment

"I can't support it if everyone who has a blog has a special privilege . . . or if Edward Snowden were to sit down and write this stuff, he would have a privilege. I'm not going to go there."
—Senator Dianne Feinstein, part-time fascist

Ever wonder how Michele Bachmann got re-elected over and over? I did. I mean, after all, she's an insane idiot. Then I thought about my own life:

I live in California. I have voted for Dianne Feinstein in the past. I didn't like it, but what else was I going to do? She's technically a Democrat, and there's never a serious primary challenger. In the Senate, keeping as many seats in the hands of Democrats is likely the only thing standing in the way of compulsory gun permits for unborn fetuses.

Outside of that narrow binary view of the world though, Sen. Feinstein is a shitty senator and a shitty Democrat. For this example, let's get some context:

In the spring of 2013, it came to light that the Justice Department (supposedly Democrat) had subpoenaed phone records of journalists and secretly obtained e-mails from journalists at Fox News. Now, domestic spying is all well and good, but spying on journalists? Something needed to be done; after all, policy-makers and the press all go to the same cocktail parties, and we wouldn't want things to get awkward. Motivations aside, the Senate Judiciary Committee got the message and actually went about the task of checks-and-balances. They wrote up a law, supposedly to protect journalists from this sort of intrusion. You'd think the first amendment would be enough, but no. Now, witness:

The final hurdle for the Judiciary Committee was defining who is a journalist in the digital era. Sen. Dianne Feinstein (D-Calif.) insisted on limiting the legal protection to "real reporters" and not, she said, a 17-year-old with his own website." I can't support it if everyone who has a blog has a special privilege . . . or if Edward Snowden were to sit down and write this stuff, he would have a privilege. I'm not going to go there," she said.

Feinstein introduced an amendment that defines a "covered journalist" as someone who gathers and reports news for "an entity or service that disseminates news and information."

"But the bill also makes it clear that the legal protection is not absolute. Federal officials still may 'compel disclosure' from a journalist who has information that could stop or prevent crimes or prevent 'acts of terrorism' or significant harm to national security."
—*LA Times*

Dianne Feinstein wants to define what a journalist is . . . which only helps define what she is.

Under this law, the First Amendment may turn out to only grant privileges rather than guarantee rights . . . which proves once again that the Constitution is a living document, because they're always trying to kill it.

Federal officials still may "compel disclosure" from a journalist who has information that could prevent crimes such as murder, kidnapping, or prevent "acts of terrorism" or acts that "significantly harm national security." Of course, this situation only arises in movies starring Ben Affleck.

The bill would protect journalists who write for newspapers and magazines, but who still reads those? She is trying to write a shield law that shields the government, not the reporter. And her backup plan is to tap the reporters' phones.

Senator Feinstein wanted the shield law to only apply to paid reporters, but Senator Charles Schumer disagreed because there wouldn't be any legal protection for writers getting screwed by the Huffington Post. See, in America, some journalists aren't paid at all, while others, especially George Stephanopoulos, are paid way too much. Meanwhile, no one has explained why Fox News is still considered journalism.

So . . . ick! This law, which is being sold as a protection for journalists, will have the opposite effect. And my Senator is fucking leading the goddamn charge down the road of good intentions.

Now look, I'm no fan of the 17-year-old blogger. For my tastes, he spends too much time talking about the cute girl in AP French. Feinstein doesn't think a 17-year-old with a website is entitled to legal protection. Fortunately, never has a 17-year-old blogger brought the government to its knees. But that's not who she's worried about anyway. She wants a law to use against Glenn Greenwald and Julian Assange.

And I'm no fan of Fox News. For my tastes, they spend too much time talking about how the cute girl will likely get pregnant just by learning French. However, my problem with those news outlets is misinformation or shitty editorial decisions. If Chad (the 17-year-old-blogger) or Fox News (the 17-year-old young-Republican-with-a-news-station) has actual information, I don't want them scared to publish it. For instance, if it turns out the cute girl from AP French is actually 18 and has a crush on me, I need that information (don't judge—I'm not made of stone).

I could assail Sen. Feinstein here endlessly, but I think *Esquire* magazine says it best:

"This is a law that redefines the exercise of a constitutional right as a privilege 'protected' by the government. This is a law that allows the government to define what 'the press' is under the First Amendment."

Let's remember something here. At the time the First Amendment was conceived, pretty much any asshole with access to a printing press could call themselves journalists. Yellow journalism abounded, and the reporting of rumors was common. There were plenty of 17-year-old bloggers at the time. Out of this maelstrom we got Thomas Paine's "Common Sense"—the pamphlet credited with fomenting the ideas of the Revolution. And this is precisely what scares Senator Feinstein.

MORE SHITTY DEMOCRATS

> **"Politicians should not engage in trying to say who should be prosecuted, or who should not. That's not a responsible thing to do."**
> **—Bill Daley, former chief of staff to President Obama, protecting Wall Street criminals from jail**

William Daley is the son of the late Chicago Mayor Richard J. Daley and is brother of outgoing Chicago Mayor Richard No-Middle-Initial Daley. What I'm saying is, he's the George W. Bush of Chicago politics—except President Bush was in the pocket of the oil industry and the military complex, where William Daley is in the pocket of the entire financial services industry.

I bet you thought I was going to say the difference was that he's a Democrat—which technically would be true, but in any meaningful way would be false—because, Wow. I mean, Wow, is this guy not a Democrat in any recognizable way.

Former banker, lobbyist, corporate attorney, and one of the architects of NAFTA—this guy actively lobbied against healthcare reform and the formation of a consumer protection bureau—two pillars of the Obama agenda.

Oh, and did I forget to mention he was the fucking White House chief of staff! From January 2011 to January 2012, this guy held one of the most powerful positions on the planet! I just pooped my pants because I said that out loud. I can't figure out which is more terrifying—that the ultimate mouthpiece for the interests who drove the economy off a cliff got the corner office to the world, or that the guy I voted for looked at his resume and said, "Yep, that's the guy I want."

So the president has surrounded himself with these types of Wall Street insiders and yet, shockingly, he hasn't reformed Wall Street. The problems that led to the market collapse in 2008 are yet to be truly addressed, because not addressing them puts money in the pockets of guys like Bill Daley. Not only that, no one has been held accountable for anything. There have been almost no criminal investigations or prosecutions of anyone in power on Wall Street at all. Here is Bill doing some non-stop lying about all this on *Meet the Press*:

> **"I think the president—No one has been more out front for the need for financial reform—"**

Let's just stop there for a second. Almost everyone has been more "out front" on the need for financial reform. Me, a nightclub comedian, has been more out front on the need for financial reform; the guy who paints house numbers on the curb in my neighborhood has been more out front on this issue . . . hell, Bernie Madoff had been more out in front on this issue.

> **"Obviously, the justice system will take its place, and the politicians should not engage in trying to say who should be prosecuted or who should not. That's not a responsible thing to do."**

Little known fact: The biggest thing Bill Daley brought with him to the Oval Office was his **extra mouth**, so he didn't have to speak out of both sides of just the one. First of all, the Department of Justice is part of the Executive Branch—and not a supposedly independent one, like the FDA or the EPA. Part of the president's job is to set an agenda for the Department of Justice—to direct them to do things. Also, in circumstances like this, in which malfeasance is obvious to even a five-year-old, if political interests might be a problem, an independent prosecutor could be appointed. Knowing this president, he'd appoint Ken Starr or Ivan Boesky. So, when Bill just said politicians shouldn't get involved, he was full-blown lying. Oh, and when he said "attorney generals are moving forward on cases that are legitimate"? Yeah, no, they're not doing that.

And what about David "I'll-never-hold-your-feet-to-the-fire" Gregory? This guy is rapidly turning into the Byron Allen of international politics. Here's some of the things that Gregory lets pass:

> **"It was tough. To be honest with you, I was in an industry that at the time, as you mention, fought many of it. Not all of it. Probably 80–85% of it the industry wanted to stop too-big-to-fail and a number of other things . . ."**

Yes, suuuurrre you wanted to end too-big-to-fail policies. Why wouldn't the people in control of two-thirds of the economy want to end a system that made them wealthy and powerful, and was essential to getting bailed out by the federal government . . . even after they sodomized the entire planet by creating and then destroying trillions of dollars in false wealth.

Of course all of them are for putting an end to "too-big-to-fail." I'm sure the guys at AIG were constantly standing around the water cooler saying, "Man, we should really break this company up into discrete and separate entities that can't completely dominate our competitors and control world-wide markets—if only there were a way!"

Of course this guy doesn't want criminal prosecutions—he's one of the criminals, and David Gregory is abetting him after the fact.

MESSAGE ON JIMMY'S VOICEMAIL:

PRESIDENT BARACK OBAMA, 2:13pm

Jimmy. This is Barack Obama. I'd like to take this opportunity to address the criticisms of my handling of this debt ceiling debate. A lot of the "professional Left" people are pissed at me because I didn't get everything they wanted in this debt negotiation.

We needed to arrive at a compromise. And as much as I hate to accept this deal, I hate standing up for traditional democratic principals and ideals even more.

Yeah, turns out. I'm kind of a pussy. But I know college kids will be happy to pay an average of 8,000 dollars more a year for graduate school rather than see us make the wealthiest Americans pay some of the bill, too. College kids appreciate the early life lesson: We live in a plutocracy run for the benefit of the very few who have bought off your government and rigged the economic game in their favor while you work your ass off to pay for it . . . AND your president is a giant pussy. Now that is a tough lesson to learn, but one I love to teach.

I've told you before, Jimmy, that you whiners on the Left have got to start acting like grown-ups. Adults. Grown-ass men.

With age we put away childish things like defending the most vulnerable. A grown-up lets the opponent frame the debate. Grown-ups do what corporations tell them to do. That's a very adult thing!

Now, I've been criticized on the left by folks who just don't want to grow up. I hear, you know, Dennis Kucinich, sucking his thumb, childishly telling us that the worker should come first. Just imagine if Martin Luther King had more of the spirit of compromise about civil rights. He might just be alive today!

So come on Jimmy, nothing and nobody are perfect. We need to meet the Republicans halfway. Everybody knows, the best way to build a bridge over a gorge is for two different parties to start on either end, build their end out, and then fasten the two together in the middle with silly string. That way everyone is safe and secure. Gimme a buzz.

DUDE, WHERE'S MY PARTY?

The only thing keeping the modern-day Tea Party-controlled Republican Party viable is that their opponents are Democrats. They've made an art out of snatching defeat from the jaws of victory.

The country is becoming increasingly progressive and will leave the current centralist Democrat Party behind.

If Democrats want to retain their base and expand the party, they have to try new strategies.

My idea is that Democrats need to start acting like Democrats. I know it sounds crazy, but it's just crazy enough to work.

We don't need a party that is slightly less Republican than the

Republicans; we need a party that is not just a little less bad as the opposition; we need a party that represents the true progressive spirit of this nation's majority. Stop listening to your well-connected big money donors (that's supposed to be what your opposition does) and start listening to the people who actually voted for you.

Maybe watch a documentary on the New Deal. Maybe glance through a biography of Franklin Roosevelt or even Teddy Roosevelt, and see how even rich people can hear the voices of the many instead of the few—if only they get the million-dollar dicks out of their ears.

Instead of sucking Wall Street cock, why not do what FDR did, and warn the people of the dangers of concentrated private power, and then vow to take them on and win. Instead we currently have Wall Street criminals not only being spared persecution, but also being rewarded with top positions in the Democratic White House.

"The liberty of a democracy is not safe if the people tolerate the growth of private power to a point where it comes stronger than their democratic state itself. That, in its essence, is fascism—ownership of government by an individual, by a group."
—Franklin D. Roosevelt

Imagine a modern-day Democrat saying that?

"We had to struggle with the old enemies of peace— business and financial monopoly, speculation, reckless banking, class antagonism, sectionalism, war profiteering. They had begun to consider the government of the United States as a mere appendage to their own affairs. We know now that government by organized money is just as dangerous as government by organized mob.

"Never before in all our history have these forces been

so united against one candidate as they stand today. They are unanimous in their hate for me—and I welcome their hatred."

Can you imagine hearing President Obama saying he "welcomes" Wall Street hate? Can you imagine how funny it would be if he did say that with Timothy Geithner, Jack Lew, Lawrence Summers, and Bob Rubin standing behind him?

And please, when it comes to foreign policy, how about offering voters an actual choice in policies instead of constantly parroting the war mongering policies of neo-cons, so you don't appear "weak"? How about the Democrats cease talking as if we can control everything that happens in the world? It's a very expensive ego trip.

In fact, if you are going to fixate on conservative ideas of cutting taxes and cutting spending, how about you start reducing the absolutely gross and astronomical amount we allocate for military spending? Because guess what? I've been told that peace is less expensive.

It seems that rank and file Democrats, as well as President Obama, never acknowledge the dark underbelly of this foreign policy. We hear the president tell us of meeting a girl at Ground Zero whose father perished in the twin towers when she was four years old, and how "getting" Bin Laden gave her closure.

And that's the real legacy of Democrat Barack Obama's foreign policy. Not peace, coalition building, or non-military solutions to conflicts, but indefinite detention without trial, indiscriminate killings via drone warfare, and heartwarming stories about the healing powers of assassination.

So my advice to Democrats is to get back to the business of being a Democrat—stand up for the little guy, the worker, the immigrant, the school teacher, and effect legislation that actually brings about a positive change in people's lives. FDR gave people jobs when they didn't have them; he gave retirement to seniors who were penniless, aid to farmers whose crops had failed, and gave people the faith to put their money in a bank again. He actually did as much for Main Street as he did for Wall Street.

And guess what happened? They elected and re-elected him until he died. The people loved him so much that after he died, they had to pass a law to limit how much people could love a president in the future.

But the Democrats are playing the same high donor game the Republicans are playing, taking in millions of campaign cash from the 1%, to use for convincing the 99% to vote for them. They have been called "Republican light," but I liken them to lite beer, they taste great, but are less filling.

Time for Democrats to go bold—embrace the New Deal again, speak about FDR the same way Republicans speak about Reagan, and demonstrate to the nation how government can work for the people instead of against them.

WHAT'S
WRONG
WITH
WALL STREET?

There are two sides of the Wall Street debate. There's the common-sense side that wants to put back the regulations that safeguarded our economy since the Great Depression until they were repealed in 1999-2000.

Unfortunately, that side doesn't have a political party representing them right now.

Then there is the side that works in the interest of the big banks that don't want to fix the problems that led to our collapsing economy. Instead, they want to make cosmetic changes that basically still allow the banks to keep doing what they've been doing and remaining too-big-to-fail. The people on that side of the debate are known as Democrats and Republicans.

And unfortunately, the news media does nothing to clear up anything or give us relevant information about potential financial reform legislation.

What sort of information? Well, for starters, how about explaining what "too big to fail" means? And then how 'bout telling us who is in favor of ending it and who isn't, and why? Or how about telling us if current legislation will keep us from the situation that led us into this mess? Does it fix the problems that we need to have fixed so that it never happens again? And why are Senators filibustering debate about regulation?

They report on Wall Street like they report on everything: like it's a soap opera, conveying the drama of events without ever giving relevant facts. Not only am I not being informed when I watch news reports about Wall Street, but I swear to God, it feels like I am somehow having information erased from my brain.

BROKEN

"In 1985, the top 5% of the households had net worth of $8 trillion, which is a lot. Today, the top five percent have

net worth of $40 trillion. . . . The top 5% have gained
more wealth than the whole human race had created prior
to 1980."
    —David Stockman, Ronald Reagan's budget director

"We're broke!"
    —John Boehner, Speaker of the House

The richest country the world has ever known, with an economy twice the size of China's, and we're broke? Sounds like Johnny's full of shit or using a Texas math book.

So how can the people who own and run the country be richer than ever, yet the country is broke? Isn't that weird? It's like the economic system is rigged or something.

We're broke! They scream, as they dismantle the few programs that still work for the people. Cut education. We're broke! Cut Social Security and Medicare. We're broke!! Cut the military. Hold on, we're not *that* broke.

Of course we are not broke. The United States has a GDP double that of China's, yet we are broke and can't afford things, and if we don't stop blowing our money on old people's medicine and teachers' pensions, we will go from broke to bankrupt, *AND THEN SHIT WILL REALLY BE SCARY!!!*

When they say we can't afford things, they don't mean things like trillion dollar wars, bank bailouts, prison construction, or billions in oil subsidies. No, they mean we can't afford things like cops, firemen, teachers, schools, Medicare, food stamps, Social Security, and anything else that actually helps people and strengthens our society.

We're not broke; in fact, we're loaded, it's just that the people in charge think that spending the money on the common good is a bad investment.

While the top 5% were gaining more wealth than the rest of the universe since the Big Bang, they were also sending your job to China, closing factories, and laying off all the people that made stuff.

See, productivity used to be tied to pay increases. That is no longer true. American worker's are waaaay more productive than they were 30 years ago. We would have 20 million more workers in the economy if we stayed at the same productivity levels we had in 1980.

So now, when workers are more productive and generate more revenue per hour worked, they generate enormous wealth for the corporations, but they get left out of their fair share of the profits. This is all happening in plain sight, day in and day out.

What we need to remember when we hear from people who have made trillions off of supply-side "Trickle-Down" economics is . . . they are full of shit. They are constantly defending a rigged economic system that has already been thoroughly debunked and discredited, except nobody seems to have told them or the American news media, and certainly not the American public.

And the biggest bullshit part of "Trickle Down" is that *if* we give massive amounts of wealth to the people *already* at the top, then a boatload of jobs will automatically appear . . . except we've been giving boatloads of money to the people already at the top since 1980, and accelerated that giving since 2000, and we are in the middle of the worst economy in 70 years. So how could that be?

If I didn't know better, I would think "Trickle Down" economics is a bunch of economic bullshit designed to enrich those who are already wealthy and screw the rest of us. But that can't be true, because this was all started by Ronald Reagan. There's the old saying, "You can't take it with you when you die." The rich who own our country don't just want to "take it with them," they want to take it *all* with them.

TRIUMPH OF THE WEILL

> **"I think that 99% of people on Wall Street are honest. They're ethical, they care about the country, they care about their shareholders . . . you always have bad apples."**
> **—Sandy Weill, man who turned investment banking into casino gambling**

You always have a few bad apples in any business . . . or as we call them on Wall Street, "chief executive officers."

If you've never heard of Sandy Weill, he's a former chairman and CEO of Citigroup. I assumed he went on TV to explain how his plan for world domination was going swimmingly until James Bond ruined everything by blowing up his secret lair. But instead he said that bullshit to make him and his criminal buddies seem likable.

You know, the kind of good people that care about feeding the poor and mentoring kids. They're such good people that it's still a mystery how they systematically and continuously bundled and sold worthless pieces of toxic paper to unsuspecting customers that cratered the housing market, wiping out retirees' wealth and collapsing an entire economy, while enriching themselves beyond their wildest dreams. Those kind of "good people."

> **"I think what we should probably do is split up investment banking from banking, have banks do something that's not going to risk the taxpayer dollars, that's not going to be too big to fail."**
> **—Sandy Weill**

Wait, a system where consumer banks are separate from investment banks?! I mean, that's fucking crazy! Except that it used to be the law—Glass-Steagall, which was instituted right after the financial crash of 1929, was designed to prevent exactly what happened in 2007, and which, get this, Sandy Weill—this guy—successfully worked to repeal during the Clinton years.

Now he's saying what most sane people have been saying since 2007. It only took the former head of Citigroup five years to get as smart as a knucklehead like me. The technical term for this is "Douchebag's Remorse."

Sandy Weill is for Glass-Steagall. In related news, Chris Christie is rethinking deep frying. When the guy who got Glass-Steagall repealed tells you Glass-Steagall needs to come back, I'm pretty sure it's time for it to come back.

And by the way—DUH!!! Go find your average idiot and explain to them what Glass-Steagall is, they'll say, "Oh yeah, we should have that." And when you further explain to that idiot—that the first de-regulating of Glass-Steagall lead to the S&L crisis in the 1980s, and later to the economic down-turn in 2007, he'll say, "Gosh, what were the smart people thinking?"

If you further tell him that the president, the secretary of the Treasury, and Congress have not so much as floated the idea of rein-stituting this law—well, that idiot's head might just explode.

LIBOR THE POINT

The too-big-to-fail banks have been manipulating global interest rates. Which isn't a big deal, except for the fact that global interest rates affect the price of *everything*.

The Libor scandal is the biggest scandal in financial history. Libor calculates and then sets the average banking interest rates. What we know now is that banks have been rigging the numbers in their favor. It has affected prices on roughly $500 TRILLION worth of financial instruments, which eventually hits local municipalities and the lives of everyday people.

When Sandy Weill was asked about the Libor scandal, he did more tiptoeing than a ballerina.

> CNBC: ". . . The Libor scandal, the idea that banks are rigging this incredibly important . . ."

> Weill: "I was very surprised; I don't think we know all the facts yet, or who did what . . ."

Ironic that the cowboy who deregulated the entire banking system now urges caution. I hear ya Sandy, let's not rush to judgment; in fact, let's move quickly in the opposite direction.

CNBC hosts usually are practiced at pretending that the guest is answering questions when they're not. But Sandy is doing such a piss-poor job that they can't. So they push back, and get a load of how Sandy Weill responds:

> CNBC: "We know that Barclays was putting in wrong bids and fake bids. They've admitted to that. Just the idea that trillions of dollars of investments are based on it [the Libor interest rate] . . ."

> Weill: "It's very unfortunate. Whatever happened, happened."

He's right. Whatever happened did indeed happen. Some people call it "rigging the system," Sandy calls it "his life's work."

If you're waiting for Sandy to say what is self-evidently true—like "criminal bankers have juiced the system for themselves while screwing over everybody else!"—you'll have to continue waiting. Remember, he said it was only a few bad apples.

And just to make us feel better before he left, Sandy gave us this:

"Believe me, we feel really bad about all the money they stole from people . . . though we are glad we'll never be punished."*

*Didn't really say this.

SHITTY MEDIA TALKS WALL STREET

"If they really are running [banks] that are so stressed that they can't do their basic work [of lending money], why are they paying themselves so much money? Where did all these enormous salaries come from if they're in so much trouble?"
—Barney Frank, *Meet the Press*

"HaHaHaHaHaHaHaHaHaHaHaHaHaHaHa!!!"
—Rest of the panel

Meet The Press September 15, 2013:
· Maria Bartiromo, CNBC
· Hank Paulson, Former Treasury Secretary
· Barney Frank, Former Congressman
· David Gregory, Tool

There are some people who wake up every day and drink the Kool-Aid. Witness here Maria Bartiromo—the pretend financial journalist and actual financial industry mouthpiece; and right beside her, former Treasury secretary under Bush junior, Mr. Hank Paulson—who, like all great regulators of the financial industry, was the CEO of Goldman Sachs for seven years. And of course, they are hosted by David Gregory, who also drinks the Kool-Aid, but just because he likes the taste and doesn't know better.

Now, what they're discussing here is the state of the banks, five years after the Lehman Brothers meltdown—a meltdown that, by the way, both of these guests had a significant hand in causing. And if you think David Gregory will ever ask them about that . . .

Also, next week, David Gregory will be interviewing the foxes about the great hen-house disaster five years later. Are the hen houses any better? We'll find out.

Yes, public favorability of the banking industry—a statistic that the last five years have shown has absolutely no meaning at all. "Wow, people don't like me and my fellow bankers? Gosh, it almost makes me not enjoy my yacht as much . . . "

But the question they are unsuccessfully trying to answer here is, *"If they are sitting on trillions of dollars, why aren't the banks lending more and investing more in the real economy?"* In response to which David Gregory shows off his stenography skills.

> **"As I talk to bankers . . . they say, 'We have to keep so much in reserve now, there's not enough capital to invest, that ultimately hurts economic growth, we're not able to make as much money, make as many deals' . . . and we have tremendous income inequality 5 years later . . . did Wall Street win in all this?"**

I like the way David Gregory just repeats what bankers have told him without ever checking 1. It's veracity, and 2. It's validity. "Oh, you guys can't invest money because of capital requirements? Doesn't sound like a claim I should check out at all—nor should I point out that those minor capital requirements were put in place because you fuckers almost destroyed the world?!"

But seriously, Maria Bartiromo, you didn't see any of this coming at all and still have massive conflicts of interest in this area—what do you think? And feel free to answer a completely different question.

"Wait, capital has doubled, and liquidity has doubled or tripled."
—Maria Bartiromo

AND . . . ? The next logical thing to explain, Maria, is why isn't that money getting invested back into the economy? And yet—

"We need to get beyond the conversation of 'Is Wall Street evil and causing pain?' and toward the conversation of 'How do we sustain growth?'"

So Maria thinks we need to get beyond "is Wall Street evil." I don't think we *need* to get beyond it—I definitely feel like I could have that conversation all day . . .

How do we create sustainable economic growth? My God, why didn't I realize that's the big deal question?!!! If only *one* domestic policymaker since the beginning of time could have thought of that question. What fools we've been!

I'm gonna flip over all of my cards and just let you know: Maria Bartiromo succeeds in saying exactly nothing here.

Sustainable economic growth will answer the question of inequality . . . you know, like it always has, right?

"Trillions of dollars are on the balance sheets . . . we need to come together and figure out how businesses, banks included, are actually going to spend that money."

Listen to what she just said: We need to come together and decide how corporations and banks are going to spend that money . . . NO, WE'RE NOT! I'm no journalist for CNBC, but I'm pretty sure *we* don't get to decide what *they* do with *their money* . . . if we did, *you* wouldn't have a fucking JOB.

The banks now have raised more money on hand, capital, than they did before the crash. Maria sees this as an *"absolute positive."*

Really? The fact that capital has been raised is an *absolute positive*? I'd say it's more of a potential positive. Until they do anything with it, it's an *absolute nothing*.

I assume they've made a Scrooge McDuck swimming pool of cash. It's what I'd do. It could also be a potential negative. I mean, how do we know the banks won't take that three trillion and buy a weather machine with which to hold the world hostage? Oh, that's right, they seem to be able to hold the world hostage without a weather machine.

And then after Maria is finished spewing empty platitudes, Hank Paulson joins in with:

> **"I couldn't agree more!"**
> **—Hank Paulson**

AGREE WITH WHAT, SECRETARY PAULSON?! She didn't fucking say anything! And then he adds on to the nothingness with another empty platitude:

> **"We need to see Democrats and Republicans coming together to deal with the big structural reforms we need."**
> **—Hank Paulson**

Look, the banks and financial services industry have paid for pretty much every president for the last twenty years. They have gotten their industry deregulated with every administration . . . so if they really want structural changes, I'm pretty sure they could get it done, which makes me think maybe they are lying when they say they are waiting on these structural changes.

At the end of the day, this is the same tired, disproven talking point over and over again: that banks and companies are waiting for certainty before they'll start re-investing in America.

Let me just say, I have sat at a lot of L.A. brunch places and overheard a lot of stupid people talking; I have smoked pot with people trying to discuss current events even though they don't own a television; I've been to Passover seders where everyone was angry and had a head injury, but this is easily one of the more stupid and circular conversations I've ever heard.

And then Barney Frank speaks up. And I'm not saying he's necessarily pulling this conversation anywhere productive, but at least he's putting the other three corporate shills in their place with a drop of common sense. If they can't lend money, then how come they can pay themselves so much goddamned money?

And it is met with a deafening SILENCE. Maria and Hank are just staring at him as if to say, "Um, that's not a serious question, right?" Even though it's the question that pretty much every American has been asking since 2008. Or maybe what their faces really mean is, "Hey Congressman Fabulous, ix-nay on the ompensation-cay, cuz if we answer that, the jig is up."

What would be great is if Barney Frank had dropped that question and Paulson had, without missing a beat, just said, "Well, because it's all bullshit—because the whole of the banking system is designed and built around a handful of people consolidating wealth and power for themselves through any means necessary—you don't think a little thing like common sense is going to get in the way of that, do you?"

HEY, ASSHOLE!–JAMIE DIMON

"We know we were sloppy. We know we were stupid; regulators should look at something like this—that's their job."
—Jamie Dimon, on losing $6.2 billion

Let me set the stage. Your car had defective brakes and crashed into a tree about five years ago. Your insurance company buys you a brand new car, which is the same car with the same brake problem. Now, the car is the economy, the insurance company is the U.S. government, the faulty brakes are credit default swaps, and you're still getting totally fucked.

Here's Jamie Dimon, the chairman and CEO of JP Morgan Chase . . . you know, one of the handful of banks that can single-handedly sink the nation's economy? Like the ones that did? Yeah, one of those. For those who don't remember, the two things that took down the economy in 2008 were toxic mortgage-backed securities and something called derivatives, or credit default swaps. Well, in May 2012, JP Morgan disclosed that they had lost over two billion dollars in the derivatives market. So, Jamie Dimon had spent the last week in almost non-stop message control. And when you want to control the message, as always, the best place to go is *Meet the Press*, where David Gregory will let you make long-winded, self-serving statements, and then pretend to challenge you for a few seconds. Here's Dimon from that interview:

"We need solutions. You know, finger-pointing, scapegoating, yelling and screaming I've never seen fix something . . ."

You know who else is against finger-pointing? Criminals. In fact, there is a new organization called "Stop the Finger-Pointing," headed by Bernie Madoff.

Yeah, I agree, finger-pointing, scapegoating, and screaming won't fix the problem. You know what will? Appropriately assigning responsibility and administering proportional punishment so that reckless and greedy assholes know they can't get away with this bullshit. Don't worry, Jamie—it's not gonna happen. I'm just saying, it would be nice.

I like how he uses "We" when he says, "We need solutions."

Really, Jamie, "We"? Oh, you're in this with the rest of us, Jamie? That just seems weird to me that *we* need solutions, when *you* created the problem. I got a pretty good solution for you: Stop fucking around with credit default swaps—that's from the you-touched-the-stove-once-and-now-you-know-not-to-do-that school of economics. It's a little complicated, I know.

But he really wants "solutions"! You know, the kind that don't involve regulation or reforming the system, or investigating those responsible. By solutions, he means keeping everything the exact same way it's always been.

DIMON A DOZEN

By the way, the week after the $6 billion loss was revealed, the board of JP Morgan voted to keep Dimon on as both chairman and CEO with his $23 million pay package intact. I assume because Jamie Dimon has photos of each board member having gay sex with every other board member. Because if that's not the case, it would mean the spirit of corporate and official responsibility is completely dead—and that would be crazy!

Twenty-three million a year. 23 million! Nobody is worth that kind of money. Okay, maybe Ryan Seacrest.

Twenty-three million and he lost 6.2 billion? Wow, I've lost money in my life, but nowhere near 6.2 billion, but then again, I'm not an expert. $6.2 billion? *you* gotta get an MBA to lose that kind of money.

Oh, and Ina Drew—the executive who directly oversaw this debacle (with full knowledge of her superiors)—will be retiring to the pile of money she's made over the years; she was one of the highest paid officers at JP Morgan. And, to boot, she likely will get a $14 million retirement package. It's like she's a public school teacher. Also, I still don't get what all those Occupy Wall Street people were going on about.

Can you imagine what the conversation with Ina Drew, the executive in charge of financial risk, was like?

Trader: "Hey Ina, we have a deal here that might lose a little money, like a couple hundred million?"

Ina Drew: "How many hundred million?

Trader: "Oh I don't know, like 60 hundred million."

Ina Drew: "Will it affect my 1.2 million a month or my 14 million retirement?"

Trader: "No?"

Ina Drew: "Then go ahead, who wants lunch?"

And . . . scene.

(Now back to our regularly scheduled outrage over Jamie Dimon already in progress.)

We need solutions, not blame? That's like the chief of police saying, "Look, we don't need to find and stop this serial killer; we need a way to stop these killings." Let me translate Mr. Dimon's little piece of sophistry. What he means is, "Look, taking responsibility for this isn't going to help; we need to figure out how we're going to get our money back!" The mob is run better than this. If this guy were a Gambino, he would have accepted that money was gone forever, and he would be dead.

Thank goodness David Gregory is there to put this one back on track.

"But what about accountability?"

Boo-yah! Yeah! What about accountability?! Go get 'em, D-Greg!

"I mean, you know, there are the stories about the bank fees—you know, the ATM fees being passed onto consumers. More regulation? Well it's going to be passed on to the consumer."

Aaaand . . . you lost me. Bank fees? ATM fees? This guy has Jamie Dimon in front of him and he asks about ATM FEES? He could have Don Corleone in front of him, and he'd ask about olive oil.

This is like a drunken conversation. Like you were just making a complex point about the dangers of supply-side economics, and David Gregory goes, "Yeah—and what's the deal with no double coupons at my grocery store?!"

How about a system based on fraud that ended up cratering our economy so we are now firing teachers, cops, and firemen, and kicking returning war heroes out of their houses? How about that? ROBO-SIGNING anyone? Does Gregory bring that up? No, that would be impolite. Gregory continues:

"You know, you hear it over and over again from critics that say, you know what? Wall Street brought down the economy; nobody's going to jail."

OK, now we're back on track. I have no idea how you expect this guy to answer this, given the fact that he's one of the people who should go to jail, and he just said he doesn't want to take responsibility—but still, whenever David Gregory gets in the ballpark, it's a minor victory. Baby steps, David, baby steps. At this rate, *Meet the Press* will be a great show for my grandchildren to watch.

How naïve of Gregory to wonder why none of the Wall Street bankers has been incarcerated. Well you know, David, jail is for people that steal thousands of dollars, not billions of dollars.

See, David doesn't seem to understand how this works, Wall Street operates outside the jail system. Jail is for the dregs of society—your drug addicts, rapists, and Martha Stewarts.

"I think there—you could say, 'these bad actors should be punished—go punish the bad actors.'"

Huh? What's Steven Segal got to do with this? Quit changing the subject.

But I am with him on that one—I saw some dinner theater the other night, and I definitely felt some punishment was in order after that production of *The Pajama Game*.

"I think that when you say that 'Wall Street'—well, I think that you're—that, that's not true. Not everyone on Wall Street was bad."

Not everyone on Wall Street was bad; come on, that's a whole street! There were many hot dog vendors and shoeshine attendants that had nothing to do with anything.

I see his point, though—you can't arrest everyone, so why arrest anyone?

Less than a minute ago, this guy was saying he doesn't want to blame anyone; he wants to find the solution. Now he's saying he wants to punish the people responsible, but that there is no underlying problem to solve. That's like a snake eating its own tail—while shaped into a Möbius strip.

Now, I just told a joke I don't even understand to express how much I don't understand this guy.

"Not all bankers are bad, not all media is bad; I like you."

Of course *you* like him; he hasn't asked you a tough question in 20 minutes, and he's lobbed you so many softballs that this interview should be on ESPN!

"So, I don't like this attitude of just blame everybody. Go get—if you think someone did something wrong, go get those people that did something wrong and blame them."

No shit, CEO of one of the largest banks in the world. I can't believe it, either. Besides talking like "Joe, The Blue-Collar Guy Who Has a Lot to Say," his statements betray fairly two-dimensional thinking. For instance, he's incapable of understanding that maybe the policies and culture of Wall Street are what made it possible—if not likely—that bad actors would eventually wipe out hundreds of billions of dollars of wealth. Also, Captain Best and Brightest here seems to have trouble with the complexities of, say, it's not an either/or situation. See, we can punish greedy, reckless douchebags *and* say Wall Street sucks balls at the same time.

"In the meantime, the rest of us should hold hands, get together, collaborate."

Yes, that's what we should do. Get a really good arts commune going.

"Business and government together. Fix the problem. It's going to be very hard for government to do it on its own. And business can't do it without collaborating with the government."

I would be willing to see how government does on its own. I mean totally free of lobbying and corporate financing of national campaigns. I'm pretty sure business can do it on its own, too—it just won't be as easy, what with the government passing laws that consistently favor big business and giving out fat government contracts and bailing out the banks and protecting asshole Bank bosses like you from being murdered in the streets by an angry mob of well-informed people.

WHY DO WE HATE JAMIE DIMON?

Jamie Dimon is the president and CEO of JP Morgan Chase, which is one of the top four banks in the U.S. It used to be one of the top nine, but we as a nation all agreed we needed to consolidate our "too-big-to-fail" banks.

He also sits on the Board of Directors of the New York Federal Reserve . . . and there's no way that might be a conflict of interest that speaks to a systemic problem of money influencing government. He's held these two positions since before the recession of 2008.

So why do we hate Jamie Dimon more than all of the other investment bankers who stayed rich while they tanked the economy? Why is he the bluest Smurf? Well, the Obama administration has held up Jamie as an example of what a great manager should be.

Democrats and Republicans alike in both the House and Senate love this guy. To hear these guys gush, you'd swear he hot-tubs with them every weekend. Jamie Dimon has taken this incredible influence and goodwill and used it to fight every common-sense financial regulation that has ever been.

So, maybe the question shouldn't be Why Do We Hate Jamie Dimon? Maybe the question should be Why Do Policymakers Love Him?

BLANKFIEN AND OTHER SWINE

"You're going to have to undoubtedly do something to lower people's expectations . . . the entitlement and what people think they're going to get because they're not going to get it. Social Security was not devised to be a system that

supported you for a 30-year retirement after a 25-year career. The retirement age has to be changed; maybe some of the benefits have to be affected, maybe some of the inflation adjustments have to be revised, but in general, entitlements have to be slowed down and contained."
   —Lloyd Blankfien, billionaire, CEO Goldman-Sachs, letting us know there isn't enough pie for us

CBS News decided to do a story on the deficit, what the problems are, and how we can fix them. And who better to help us understand the problems of our debt and deficit than a billionaire banker who stuffed his pockets full of cash while helping bankrupt the treasury?

And guess what he sees as the big problem with the deficit. Is it unpaid for tax cuts for millionaires and billionaires?

Nope.

Is it the 80 billion dollars the Federal Reserve gives to Wall Street for free every month in the form of "quantitative easing"?

Nope, that's not it.

So what does one of the heads of Wall Street think is the problem with our debt?

It's these fucking old people who worked all their life and now want to retire and expect Social Security to give them $660 a month of the money they paid into it. I knew it wasn't Wall Street and outsourcing of jobs to slave labor, I just knew it!

Plus he provides us with some outrageously compelling and completely made-up statistics to back up his bullshit.

"30-year retirement after a 25-year of career" . . . so wait a minute, someone retires after 25 years of work? So he is saying the problem is all those people who start working at 40 years old? I've never met anyone like that, but according to his totally bullshit argument, there are tons of them. And the reporter lets it fly right by.

"Times have changed . . ." Yeah, times have changed, Lloyd; it's not like the old days when you retired at 65, and a few weeks later your heart exploded. Now these assholes work their whole lives and then don't die right away. These are really fucked up times.

I don't blame him for being annoyed; these deadbeats who've spent their whole lives just scraping by want to retire on money that belongs to hard-working billionaires. It seems like Lloyd's theory is that if you explain to people that the government will no longer pay for their old age, you can mentally prepare them to die a lot sooner than they expected. Savings, savings, savings!

"We're going to have to do something to lower people's expectations . . ."

Yeah, It's about time we put the responsibility where it belongs . . . on the people who should've made more money.

"Social Security was not devised to be a system that supported you with a 30-year retirement . . ."

So his point is that we just can't keep wasting Social Security on all these 95-year-olds!

Is that really a big drain on the Treasury? Is all the Social Security being eaten up by the 90-year-olds? Well, as of 2006 there were 1.9 million people over 90 years of age in the U.S., and they suck up a little over a billion in Social Security a year. That's billion with a B! Or roughly a little less than we spend in Afghanistan per week. So can you see the dilemma that kids in the future will deal with? Are we going to support our Americans over 90, or cut out a whole week of fighting in the Middle East? Talk about Sophie's Choice.

"The retirement age has to be changed . . ."

Yeah, we should raise the retirement age to say, 67, 70, 89 . . . we'll save a fortune on gold watches for retirement.

Just so we are clear on how off the mark he is, consider that most people who actually work for a living aren't living longer. Since 1977, those in the upper half of income have seen their life expectancy expand by six years, while those in the bottom half have gained only 1.3 years.

So it turns out that once again, the often-repeated talking point of Social Security going bankrupt because people are collecting benefits for thirty years is wrong. Not just wrong, but completely wrong. And guess who it is wrong in favor of? The working class? Nope. Turns out the often-repeated incorrect assumption favors the really rich guys like bank chairmen and millionaire TV news readers.

Or as Ezra Klein put it:

"If you're wealthy, you do have many more years to enjoy Social Security. But if you're not, you don't. And so making it so people who aren't wealthy have to wait longer to use Social Security is a particularly cruel and regressive way to cut the program."

The other thing to consider is that most people who rely on Social Security had jobs that were physically demanding, and they literally cannot perform them any longer. Again, Ezra Klein explains:

"Sixty-five is the law's standard retirement age. Most people begin taking Social Security benefits at 62, which is as early as the law allows you to take them.

"When they do that, it means they get smaller benefits over their lifetime. We penalize for taking it early. But they do it anyway. They do it because, unlike many folks in finance or in the U.S. Senate or writing for the nation's

op-ed pages, they don't want to work 'til they drop."

"So that is what makes their lies so insidious; they hurt the people who are the most vulnerable. The people who most need that program are going to be further burdened by people who least need it."

Lloyd Blankfien's annual salary is $55 million, his net worth is $450 million, and his company has received over $10 billion dollars in TARP from U.S. taxpayers.

So, as Klein put it, rich guys like Blankfien are "bravely advocating for a cut they will never feel." A real profile in courage.

It turns out, having all the money in the world *does not* build character.

The other 'expert' that CBS News interviewed was the CEO of Honeywell, aka a defense contractor, aka gets most of their money from the government, aka another multi-millionaire:

"The big nut is going to have to be Medicare and Medicaid . . . at the end of the day, you can't avoid the topic, especially with the baby boomer generation retiring; it's going to literally crush the system."
—David Cote, chairman of Honeywell, defense contractor

The big nut is not defense, remember that. It's not two unfunded wars and the Bush tax cuts that are crushing our system, because wars and tax cuts never crush anything; the only thing with the power to crush things is healthcare for the elderly, remember that.

What he's really saying is that Medicare is raiding our military budget . . . so if we go on trying to keep people alive, we won't have enough money to kill people! I get it now.

I mean, let's be brutally honest, between a decrepit aircraft carrier or your grandmother, which one can be retrofitted?

"It's going to literally crush the system . . . " Yeah, and if it doesn't, he'll do it himself. He'll have to do something because, if things continue like this, one day we won't even know where our next nuclear warhead's coming from.

David Cote is a sharp cookie who knows that the first rule of business is you have to pick the battles you can win, and this is a definite "win" for all the defense contractors, because elderly sick people can't fight back that hard.

Thank God CBS News decided to ask a bank chairman and a defense contractor what the problems are with our debt and deficit. It turns out what is bankrupting our country is the government spending that those guys can't get their hands on. If I were a cynic, I would call these two guys criminal assholes. But I'm an optimist, so I choose to believe they will all die and come back as Mel Gibson's girlfriend, or worse, Joe Scarborough's co-host.

GREENSPAN STILL WRONG ABOUT EVERYTHING

"There is a general view out there that some-how we are gonna solve this [economic col-lapse] without pain; there is no conceivable scenario in which that is true. Cutting govern-ment spending will cause some retraction in economic activity, and according to the IMF . . . increasing taxes curtail economic activity, so do expen-diture cuts, but significantly less."
—Alan Greenspan, captain of the U.S. economy, who definitely did not "go down with the ship"

Here's a question: Why the fuck do we keep asking the people who created this economic crisis how to fix this economic crisis? And why do we listen to them when they suggest the exact same things they were saying before?

And yet, here's Alan Greenspan—easily one of the top five people most directly responsible for the economic meltdown. Presumably the next guest will be a Mexican druglord on how he suggests we fix the entire Juarez bugaboo.

By the way, Greenspan is citing an assessment from the IMF, an organization which has consistently sided with banks over people. It's sort of like begging the question—but closer to sexually pleasuring the question.

When is everyone going to get that Alan Greenspan is *not* an objective economist? He, by his own admission, comes to his understanding of the economy from a deep objectivist philosophy (not to be confused with actually being objective). It's the philosophy of Ayn Rand, and pretty much every entitled asshole I've ever met. Yeah, this is the "Greed is Good" thought process—which, by the way, Greenspan came by honestly when he was Ayn Rand's lover, which, if you've seen either of these people—ick. Man, she must have been some lover, because I, for one have never sexed someone so good that it altered her worldview.

To be fair, I've certainly sexed a few girls poorly enough to make them really question some basic assumptions.

My point is, Greenspan comes into every discussion of the economy wanting certain things to be true—that low taxes and less regulation make the world into a magical wonderland where everyone gets to live out their dreams.

Let's take one more look at his prescription for economic recovery.

"There is a general view out there that somehow we are going to solve this [economic collapse] without pain; there is no conceivable scenario in which that is true."

See what he did there, he said that for sure, definitely, no doubt about it, he's 1000% certain that there will be pain for people in order for us to get out of this mess. But then says:

> **"Cutting government spending will cause some retraction in economic activity, and according to the IMF . . . increasing taxes curtail economic activity, so do expenditure cuts, but significantly less."**

Great, more tax cuts for millionaires, and the rest of us can go pound sand.

Remember all that inevitable pain he was talking about? Turns out only the working class and the poor need to feel any pain to get us out; once again Greenspan found a way to spare the rich any pain, damage, responsibility, or consequence for anything. When I hear objectivist philosophers get everything wrong, my philosophy objects to it.

SHITTY MEDIA—MARIA BARTIROMO STYLE

> **"Markets are built on confidence . . . they need to have confidence that there is a plan that will encourage businesses to create jobs."**
> **—Maria Bartiromo, CNBC business reporter**

That's one of those Republican talking points disguised as common sense—as sung by the mynah bird of financial journalism, Maria Bartiromo. She is a Wall Street stenographer and mouthpiece. Sorry, I mean she's a CNBC business reporter who reports from the economic trenches. In fact, she is actually embedded with a squadron of criminally insane CEOs, last seen storming the beaches of East Hampton Long Island with Wall Street's 82nd douchebag division.

I don't think Maria has a penis, but she definitely has a huge set of balls saying that load of empty drivel. Corporations are not investing or hiring but are sitting on five trillion dollars, and Maria says it's because they lack "confidence." Hey, if five trillion dollars doesn't give you confidence, I'd try dance lessons.

Pretty much since President Obama was elected, Republicans have been claiming that the economy is stalled because businesses won't expand if they don't know what's going to happen next. They claimed it with the healthcare debate, and now they're claiming it with tax policy . . . and it's total and complete bullshit. Businesses hold off expansion when they don't see a market to sustain expansion. That's why you don't see huge dream catcher factories.

But wait! This president put out a 700 billion dollar stimulus bill—a plan specifically to create jobs—and Republicans went crazy. He's pushing another 400 billion dollars in stimulus, and the Republicans are crapping all over him.

And by the way—yes, confidence is a crucial element of the markets. But guess what? The private sector is sitting on roughly two trillion dollars and isn't investing in the future. A few years ago, the private sector was investing like crazy—very confident—but with no capital to back up those investments. I'm just saying, maybe a little less confidence is appropriate.

If a friend was drunk and wiped out his motorcycle, Maria Bartiromo would conclude he doesn't want to get back on that motorcycle because he's anticipating a rise in gas prices. The point here is, don't be friends with Maria Bartiromo, because that will be an awkward hospital visit.

She never asks a real question of anybody because, even though she is an economic reporter, she doesn't understand economics or how to ask a good question.

"They need the government to give them some certainty, some clarity, so that business can actually put plans

together for 2013 in terms of hiring plans," stated Maria Bartiromo, business reporter/dipshit.

"I totally agree," responded Andrea Mitchell, MSNBC professional know-nothing.

Oh yeah, Wall Street needs certainty, like the certainty JP Morgan Chase has when they lose billions of dollars and nobody in the company gets busted. Yes, Maria Bartiromo does seem like she's full of crap, but that's only because we're not Andrea Mitchell.

The only thing Wall Street hates more than uncertainty is telling the truth. And how do they know that it is uncertainty that is keeping corporations from hiring? Because they asked CEOs and Wall Street criminals (in Andrea's case, she also asks the former Fed Chairman Alan Greenspan, who was so good at his job he silently watched as the U.S. economy deregulated the banks and drove slowly of a cliff), and they all keep saying "Certainty! We need certainty!"

Do they ever ask anyone else besides multi-millionaires who are looking for more tax breaks? Like Paul Volcker? Or Paul Krugman? Or anyone named Paul?

They sure didn't ask Mark Haines of CNBC. He was the last of the real reporters who questioned Wall Street and CEOs, instead of repeating their talking points. Here Mark Haines clears up this "business-needs-confidence-and-certainty" canard:

"It has nothing to do with confidence; companies hire when they see more demand for their goods and services, period, the end. When business picks up, they hire—if business doesn't pick up, they don't hire."

I would love to play that on a projection screen outside of Maria Bartiromo's apartment window at full volume for a month.

HEY, ASSHOLE!—CHARLES PAYNE

"Don't think that the Bangladeshi people who perished
didn't want or need those jobs . . . I know we like to victimize everyone in this country, particularly when it comes to
for-profit motivation, which is being assaulted. But, I think
it is . . . an amazing stretch, to pin this on Wal-Mart. The
unions in this country are desperate."
  —Capitalism spokesman Charles Payne, reacting to a
    factory fire in Bangladesh that killed 112 workers after
    mangers ordered workers back to their stations when
    the fire alarm went off

When a clothing manufacturer "outsources" its production and jobs
to a third-world country, it means they can make boatloads more
money if they stop paying their workers a living wage and send their
jobs to a country without the hassles of government regulations that
keep workplaces safe.

It's the new American way: We screw our own citizens out of
good-paying jobs by turning them into shitty jobs and shipping
them overseas.

So in one of the factories that makes our clothes with slave
labor and no workplace protections, there was a fire that killed
112 people.

People with a conscience reacted to this tragedy by contemplating
the true price of things. Luckily, people without a conscience had
Charles Payne to represent them.

I want to go over Charles Payne's statement to better understand it.

"I don't think something like this will happen again . . ."

Huh? This factory might as well invite Great White to come play, because as long as people can still get Nikes for twenty bucks, there ain't gonna be sprinkler systems in these labor mills.

"Don't think those people in Bangladesh who perished didn't want or need those jobs as well. . . ."

AAAAAAHHHHH!!! That's the point, you myopic fuck! People who desperately need jobs will put up with conditions they should not. It's their desperation that is being exploited.

"You know, I know we like to victimize everyone in this country, especially when it comes to the for-profit motivation which is being assaulted in this country—"

Man, that is so true! Capitalism is such a victim here. When will people stop victimizing large, highly profitable multi-national corporations? Those people have feelings too . . . unfortunately none of those feelings are basic human decency—but still.

"You know, it's a tragedy, but I think it's a stretch—an amazing stretch, to try to sort of pin this on Wal-Mart . . ."

I don't know if it's that much of a stretch . . . . I mean, I know it's a complex web, but let me see if I can connect the dots:
– Wal-Mart hires Company X to make clothes for cheap because it is located in Bangladesh, where workers can be paid shit with no safety protections.
—Because they have no safety standards, Company X has a fire. Wow. That was a lot fewer dots to connect than I expected.

"I'm not here as an apologist for Wal-Mart—"

Good thing you said that, cuz it sounded so much like an apology up 'til now.

"But I am here as something—as a spokesperson for capitalism and the American Dream, and I think for a lot of people, this is a step in the right direction—"

What the fuck?! What is a step in the right direction? Roasting garment workers? What direction do you think is right—a direction in which we can all accept burned human beings as just the cost of doing business? This could just be me, but I don't think that's a good direction.

And this guy is called a spokesman of capitalism and the American Dream? Someone should have interviewed more applicants before appointing him. This guy is the spokesman for the American Dream in the same way George Zimmerman was a neighborhood watch captain.

THE EXPENSIVE FREE MARKET

The idea of a free market is bullshit. It is one of those things that never was, yet some people think it has always been, but it hasn't, cuz it isn't and it never was.

When economists speak of free markets, they are referring to economies where consumers can choose products and services uncoerced, and prices aren't set by the government. But lots of people think it means completely unregulated capitalism. No regulation at all, zero, nada, nil, zilch. But that's not what it means.

These same type of people talk about the free market as if it was invented by Jesus or something, and is therefore the most moral way to run an economy. Literally, they equate capitalism with morality.

Do you know these people? To them, the free market means no government regulation, and any regulation on business transactions must

be immoral. This kind of thinking leads these same nitwits to the conclusion that other forms of economies are somehow inherently evil.
Not figuratively evil, but LITERALLY evil, like FROM THE DEVIL evil.

We hear them speak about the free market as if it had existed in
nature somewhere, and humans stumbled upon it, and so we use it
in the United States, because this is Jesus' favorite country, and he'd
wanted us to have it. To these people they see any regulation as
unnatural or artificial—a perversion of nature. And in their heads,
perversion sounds like sex, so they think it has to be a sin.

What these people fail to understand is that there is no such
thing as a FREE MARKET. It doesn't exist in any form anywhere. All
markets are regulated. The only ones that aren't are run by pirates.

And markets, all markets, are invented by humans to serve their
societies, not the other way around. Markets are here to *serve us*; we
are not here to serve them. And if a market we invented to serve us
isn't doing such a good job anymore, we can change the market!

A lot of those same people make the mistake of equating democracy with capitalism. They are not the same thing. Capitalism is just
one form of an economy, just like democracy is one form of government. In a democracy, people get to choose the kind of economy
they want, and in America we chose capitalism. REGULATED capitalism.

Regulations, good regulations, help economies run and work
better. If we didn't have effective regulations on Wall Street, the
bankers could create serial bubble after serial bubble and crash our
economy. But who would be stupid enough to allow that to happen?

In fact, it turns out that regulating business is the RESPONSIBIL-
ITY of government. The Supreme Court in the *Munn* decision said:

**"Property does become clothed with a public interest when
used in a manner to make it of public consequence, and**

affect the community at large. When, therefore, one devotes his property to a use in which the public has an interest, he, in effect, grants to the public an interest in that use, and must submit to be controlled by the public for the common good . . ."

That means that if you want to do your business in and around my community or do business that will affect others . . . like giving them cancer, or asthma, or causing all the fish to die and the beaches to turn black . . . well then, those others get to have a say in your business through our elected representatives.

And guess what? Everybody is for regulation—it's just a matter of how much. Don't believe me? Then you think it is okay for someone to advertise a product for one price but change it when the person gets to the store? Or how about six-year-old children mining coal, is that cool? Or getting orange-flavored grout when you thought you purchased shaving cream? Or unknowingly wearing clothes made of Strychnine? Or buying a computer that doesn't include an eleven-year-old to assemble it?

So, we're all for regulation. Of course, I could be totally wrong about the economics I spewed here, but those people who are against regulated markets still bug the fuck out of me. If only gasoline had more lead in it.

DIVERGING

Nothing puts my teeth on edge more than hearing scruffy-chinned college students blaming corporations for every ill in the world. Mainly because they have a point.

In the United States, corporations are, legally speaking, people. The main reason for this legality is for protecting employees, officers, and investors from direct litigation. It's actually an important construct for successful capitalism. Unfortunately, this has turned corporations into autonomous entities not unlike Frankenstein's monster (from the movie, not the book).

Corporations have a single purpose: profit.

In the case of publicly owned corporations, the drive toward profit is amped to dangerous levels. After all, if a company fails to meet profit expectations, the share values might plummet, and the whole thing could fall apart, thus depriving a vice president of another jet. So quarter after quarter, the monster gets hungrier and hungrier.

One might say that a corporation will do anything legal to make money, but this wouldn't be entirely accurate. Corporations routinely calculate the costs of illegal and unethical activities, and if the profits exceed the malfeasance, then scum-baggery it is! Remember, corporations are amoral entities by design.

Adding to this problem is our political system—which I hear is more than a little vulnerable to influence. Most congressmen will easily admit that they spend at least as much time raising campaign funds as they do congressional business. Even local elections have become dangerously expensive affairs. After the McCain/Feingold Act, which limited individual contributions, the only source of serious campaign funds became large corporations. And so here we are.

On one hand, we have giant, amoral companies constantly pursuing their limited interests—on the other hand, we have politicians eagerly pursuing huge mountains of campaign cash. The only thing that stops these companies from polluting the air and water, exploiting its workers, and kicking puppies is the federal government.

Anyone see a problem here? So now, liberal or conservative, every candidate has to take corporate money from the very companies that they'll have to later regulate. In a strange coincidence, pretty much every serious regulatory agency has been slowly shrunk over the last thirty years.

Nothing I've just written is a big mystery. As I pointed out earlier, filthy hippie college students can figure it out over bong hits. Do you know who else figured it out? Pat Buchanan! Pat FUCKING Buchanan, the goodest, oldest good ol' boy of all time. The guy who can deny evolution and be racist in one sentence. For real, here's what Buchanan said on *Morning Joe*:

> "It's a simple fact that the interests of corporate America and the interests of the country have diverged. If General Electric is building plants in the United States, that's good for America. But if they're going to make themselves more efficient by shutting down a plant here and opening it up in China or Mexico or somewhere else, that may be good for G.E. and its shareholders, stockholders like me—but it is not good for America; it is not good for the workers of America, and that's what's killing these unions. It's Republicans as well as Democrats who are in the back pocket of the business roundtable, authorizing them to go abroad and produce there, and export free to the United States of America."

Can you believe that? It was accurate and concise. After I heard that clip, I thought I had been kidnapped by aliens and put into an alternate reality experiment. But no . . . sadly no. Funny how on *Morning Joe*, they take turns being straightforward and rational for a segment or two, but never all at the same time.

OK, exact same show, moments later, Jack Welch gets to talk. For those of you who don't know, Jack Welch is the real-life Gollum. I would not be surprised if it comes out that he was a G.E.-manufactured puppet turned into a real boy by the power of greed. That boy then grew up to be a million years old and run G.E. from 1981 to 2001. Since then, he's become one of the most vocal defenders of unchecked capitalism in the U.S. Here's his two cents on the matter:

"... look, I think in general, if G.E. didn't move—or G.M, I.B.M., or anybody else, if you don't be competitive, no consumer in America says, 'Let me see, I'm gonna buy this refrigerator or something from G.E., cuz it's made here, even though it costs a hundred dollars more than the one from Samsung or the one from L.G.' ... If G.E. stays in these high-cost plants and makes something and says 'I made it for America! Buy it!' [the American people will say] 'Sorry, I'm taking the one next to it.'"

Unfortunately, he's right, too. Capitalism depends as much on the amorality of consumers as the amorality of companies. The overwhelming evidence is that American consumers will buy the slave labor shirt from God-knows-where because it's three dollars cheaper than the semi-slave-labor shirt from right here in the Good Old U.S. of A-holes.

What Jack Welch isn't saying is that appropriate regulatory, trade, and tax laws could solve many of the problems caused by outsourcing. We could, for example, make it illegal to sell goods in this country which have been made by slaves. Wouldn't that be nice? We could also restructure our corporate tax law so that a company like G.E. can't hide billions of dollars overseas. Of course, none of this will happen, because G.E. and all the rest of the large multinational corporations pay for U.S. elections.

So, to be fair, we hate corporations at least as much as all the public officials who've been coerced out of their fiduciary responsibilities. And to be fair to most Americans, economically speaking, they don't have a choice in what products they can purchase, with their jobs paying so little because of competition with overseas corporate plantations.

So, when President Obama—a guy I voted for twice, a guy the Right routinely calls a socialist—when this president says things like this, I get a little irked:

"... that is, we act like grown-ups. And when we are in negotiations like this, that everybody gives a little bit, compromises a little bit, in order to do the people's business."

That's a statement he made from the debt ceiling negotiations . Unfortunately, but not surprisingly, the "compromises" to which the president is alluding are public entitlements; particularly Social Security and Medicare. You know, the things that aren't important at all and no one likes.

Moving on, the following week President Obama said this during his State of the Union address:

"The stock market has come roaring back. Corporate profits are up. The economy is growing again."

So then why do we have to cut Social Security? Seems that if the economy is down, then we have to cut Social Security. But if the economy comes "roaring back," then we still have to cut Social Security.

And the fact that the stock market came roaring back would have been comforting if it weren't for the fact that, in 2008, we learned that most of the stock market is just pretend. Still, can't hate profits; can't hate a growing economy. That means a more stable tax base, so we can pay for things like Social Security and Medicare, right?

They say the Great Recession officially ended in 2009, yet the economy stagnates with worrying unemployment levels, fewer people participating in the workforce, and incomes which are decisively lower than before the economic crash.

A recent report from Sentier Research found that the median annual household income of Americans is getting lower and lower after every successive quarter. For many Americans, incomes aren't just stagnant, they're falling—along with their purchasing power and standard of living.

So, just to be clear: corporate profits up; the lower and middle class, down. And as that is happening, our president is talking about giving away entitlements (which, by the way, aren't entitlements—you pay into Social Security just as you pay into Medicare).

Did I mention they keep calling this guy a socialist?

JACK, ASS

"Large, publicly owned corporations are insane criminals, and our government is abetting their crimes."
—me

Remember how former G.E. President Jack Welch was defending outsourcing? OK, keep that in mind. The other part of outsourcing, the less obvious part, is moving a corporate headquarters overseas. Actually, not really moving the headquarters overseas, but moving certain legal entities to different countries in order to avoid United States corporate taxes. Look, I'm not an accountant (according to my wife, I'm barely a man), so I can't explain the exact mechanisms, but the result is obvious:

"Such strategies, as well as changes in tax laws that encouraged some businesses and professionals to file as individuals, have pushed down the corporate share of the nation's tax receipts—from 30% of all federal revenue in the mid-1950s to 6.6% in 2009 . . . At 35%, the corporate tax rate is nominally among the world's highest. Yet because of 'a bounty of subsidies, shelters, and special breaks,' most companies actually pay less than competitors abroad—often far less."

Yeah, no kidding. So, just to be clear, these companies exist here.

Their corporate officers are here. A huge share of their profits are made here. However, they have moved their lowest paying jobs overseas; removing them from the American economy. Also, they've moved as much of their tax revenue away from the United States as possible. It's like they're still living with their parents, but refusing to pitch in for the groceries or even be nice to their mom.

But let's get back to G.E.:

According to the *New York Times* story, G.E. reported U.S. profits of $5.1 billion in 2010 (and $14.2 billion worldwide). "What is its American tax bill?" asked the *Times*. "None. In fact, G.E. claimed a tax benefit of $3.2 billion." The company accomplished this by "an aggressive strategy that mixes fierce lobbying for tax breaks and innovative accounting that enables it to concentrate its profits offshore."

And I will take a break from writing to scream and throw things . . . and we're back. If you didn't think this couldn't get more infuriating, consider this:

G.E. makes a huge percent of their domestic profits from GOVERNMENT CONTRACTS. General Electric makes shit like jet fighter engines and nuclear triggers. In 2010, the United States government paid G.E. over $3 billion, and yet they don't have the basic decency to pay their taxes. That's just impolite.

G.E. is just one example—an egregious one to be sure—as this is a systemic problem. But if you ever hear a conservative claiming they are an isolated case, you have my permission to punch them in the balls.

Now . . . if you're not already dangerously furious, let's add another layer:

A survey also found a majority of Republicans and independents favor cutting government spending over raising taxes on businesses, while Democrats are evenly divided.

Yup, as we've said before, large corporations get government to do their business through lobbying, campaign finance, and other tricks of influence. In this case, policy makers have become corporate officers in charge of lowering the expense of taxes. For example, here's Senator Ron Johnson, Republican from Wisconsin, on the matter of G.E.'s 0 percent effective tax rate:

"We have to be concerned about what the business environment is in the U.S. here. I mean, we can't afford to have the highest tax rate in the world. I mean, we have got to make America a very attractive place for business investment. You know, it's not like we have a choice to compete; we have to compete globally. So we've got to bench-mark our tax rates, our regulatory environment, against the world if we expect to have this economy growing. And let's face it, in order to get out of this budgetary hole, the number one solution is economic growth."

And then, the good senator was asked, ". . . on tax reform for corporations, what rate do you think you have to bring it down to actually get, to become competitive, in that when you look at a company like G.E., the effective tax rate is 0?"

And his response:

"Again, those are individual companies. I think overall, we really can't be looking at a corporate tax rate higher than 25%, because that's kind of the world average. So, you know, we're sitting up there at 35%, and that's just the wrong signal, and we've gotta create a competitive environment here in the U.S."

It is clear this isn't just a problem of "individual companies." However, by claiming it's not a pervasive problem, the senator doesn't have to address the real question: how do you get companies to pay even close to the taxes they should?

And should major corporations be paying 35%? Here are just a few of the benefits a company gets by operating in the United States: our stable and strong currency, highways, ports, law enforcement, education, and the protections of the largest military in the world. It seems like a pretty equitable deal to me. In fact, it seems pretty fucking competitive. But they're not even paying close to 35%; in G.E.'s case, they're not paying anything. I'm no math whiz, but I'm pretty sure if we drop the corporate tax rate as the senator demands, we would all end up paying G.E. just to exist.

Pardon me while I wave my American flag made in China.

WHAT'S
WRONG
WITH
GOD?

There was a review released consisting of 63 studies of intelligence and religion, which revealed that people who don't believe in God are smarter than people who do. The results are provocative, but less so for religious people, because they don't know what the word "provocative" means.

Researchers studied a century of intelligence tests, as well as the history of Pakistan and the speeches of Rick Santorum. Atheists consistently scored higher than religious people on IQ tests, although they often spoiled it by being smug.

The research suggested atheists spend more time in school and get higher-level jobs . . . while people who believe in God are less educated and don't think as rationally, which is why they buy lottery tickets.

The study also found that religious people are not as good at problem-solving . . . just try asking them why God lets bad things happen to good people. They've still got no answer for that.

However, the researchers did admit that some atheists can be stupid, while certain religious people may seem intelligent, but only because they say they're Buddhists. Overall, atheists simply don't need God as much, though even an atheist may suddenly turn to prayer several hours after eating at an ethnic street festival. Now there's a new study showing that overweight people without money have sex with anybody that will let them.

HEY, ASSHOLE!—PAT ROBERTSON

"If you can't scrape up a couple thousand bucks, there's something wrong with you."
—Pat Robertson, ministering to the poor

So there's a segment in Pat Robertson's show where he gives life advice to people who write in with their problems. It's like Dear Abby, except Abby in this case is a certifiable maniac. Here is the letter and the response that earned Pat a place in "Hey, Asshole!"

> "My mom is dying from a lung disease. She watched your show the other morning; when I arrived, she told me that you said the Bible says cremation is wrong. Well, here's the problem: mom does not have money, nor do I. So cremation is our only option.
>   "Believe me, it breaks my heart to know that she would rather be buried, and of course, that would be our first choice, but it would cost thousands of dollars we don't have. Now my mom believes it would be wrong as a Christian to be cremated. I love my mom a lot, but wouldn't it also be wrong to go into debt for years to give her a burial? What do I tell her?"
>   —Letter from *700 Club* viewer

> "I'm sure that somewhere along the way, you can find a mortician somewhere that can give you a discount burial. If you can't scrape up a couple thousand bucks, there's something wrong with you."
>   —Pat Robertson

Pat's right . . . anyone without money has to be insane!

You see, Jesus loves the poor, but not after they're dead.

Thanks, Pat, I'm sure Mom will take a great deal of comfort from that.

Probably the reason that woman's broke is she gave all her money to Pat Robertson . . . because he told her he really needed it.

You know, Pat, not everybody knows how to build a religious media empire off of other people's fear and ignorance.

Obviously, about 30 years ago Pat Robertson buried his compassion.

Billy Graham's daughter on *Meet the Press*, telling us what she looks for in a leader:

". . . the Bible says that the beginning of wisdom is fear of God. And I believe one of the greatest lacks in our nation today is that genuine fear and reverence for an Almighty God. And that's where wisdom begins . . . that's what I look for in a president. I want my leader to have a fear and a respect and a reverence for God."

Yes, if there is one thing I know for sure, it is that some of the best thinking occurs when you approach problems from a position of fear.

Once again, the conservatives reveal their Fear Fetish. They have elevated fear to a virtue, and now attribute it to great leaders:

"Hey, look at that guy. Boy, is he a good leader or what?"

"Which guy?"

"They guy over there shitting his pants, he's got what God likes in a leader."

Her father, Billy Graham, was good friends with Richard Nixon, who feared both God and the satanic Jews who ran the media.

Weird that she would say something so stupid, because when you talk to religious zealots in the Bible belt, they usually have "razor-sharp intellect."

Yeah, knowledge is all fine and good, but when mankind stopped slaughtering non-believers and started reading books, we lost something really special.

PHONE CALL WITH BILL O'REILLY,

10:47pm

JIMMY: Yello. Jimmy Dore here. And yes, I am satisfied with my long-distance carrier.

O'REILLY: Jimmaay Dore. Answer the phone for freakin' Christ. Our public schools are ignoring God!

JIMMY: I'm here, Bill. And who cares? That's what public schools are supposed to do.

O'REILLY: You're not a pagan, are you Jimmy? You don't believe in all this weird Wiccan bullshit about dead people rising from the grave, and burning incense while some lollipop dressed in silk robes goes around slap-hammering young boys, do you?

JIMMY: Of course not, Bill.

O'REILLY: Oh my God! I just described the Catholic Church! How ironic. Hoisted by my own Picard.

JIMMY: "Petard," Bill. You mean "petard," not "Picard."

O'REILLY: Are you accusing me of being drunk, Jean-Luc? Because according to Starfleet General Order #1, that is not within the scope of the Prime Directive.

JIMMY: Bill, even if I did believe in a god, it's not the job of public schools to spread religion.

O'REILLY: God is real, jagoff. For example: I am a miracle. Ya follow me? My hairline. My huge, protruding forehead, the way my face lights up like a baboon's ass whenever I'm upset or sexually aroused—these are all miracles, proof of God, Jesus Christ our Lord. And someday, after my work is done here on earth, God will call me, and I shall sit at the throne of Jesus and his pet mongoose, Sidney. In the meantime, Satan will be juggling your mom's funbags over a fire pit of burning Biebers.

JIMMY: You can't prove there's a god, Bill.

O'REILLY: Here's more proof—just doing this with my finger. What the human body has to do in order to make my finger do this is pretty miraculous, right? If there's no God, how do you explain the miracle of what I'm doing with my finger right now?

JIMMY: Okay, I'll bite. What are you doing with your finger right now?

O'REILLY: I'm flippin' you the bird, Jimmay! Flippin' you the bird. You pagan ninny-funtz. You got a good, strong back, boy. You'll need it. You and me gonna have fun, dammit. Pray with me. Say, why don't we get right down on our knees now?

JIMMY: Get down—where?

O'REILLY: Right here, Joe Buck. I prayed in the saloons, I prayed in the street, I prayed in the toilet. He don't care where, Joe. What He wants is that prayer! Gonna be like money from home, Joe Buck, money from home!

JIMMY: Bill, you're completely smashed again.

O'REILLY: I prefer to call it "getting closer to God." Uh oh. Uh oh. I feel another prayer coming on . . . "Please God, don't let me throw up again. It's a waste of Jack Daniels." (VOMITS)

CATHOLIC CONTRACEPTION

"Catholics are tired of the government and others beating up on the church."
—George Weigel, Catholic scholar

We are all tickled pink about the new direction of the Catholic Church (which reminds me of when a priest tried to tickle my pink parts, but I'll tell that story some other time). I'm overjoyed at how great Pope Francis is for putting forward the issue of inequality.

And yet, instead of tending to the poor, there's some peculiar matters in which members of the church have spared time to get involved. For example, there's a manufactured phony controversy about contraception. It's being pushed by partisan morons and some Catholic bishops who scream about condoms and cover up child rape.

Well, it turns out Catholics are being victimized again. I mean, the Obama administration is requiring them to provide comprehensive health insurance to their secular employees in hospitals and schools that would include contraceptive. Obama, you jack-booted thug!

Here is Chris Matthews, who still defers to closeted homosexuals dressed up like Elton John on matters of spirituality, asking us to listen to George Weigel, one of his favorite scholars on Catholic Studies.

"This has struck a tribal nerve in Catholicism. The Catholic Church has been beaten up for the last ten or eleven years; Catholics are tired of the government and others beating up on the church."
—George Weigel, Catholic Scholar, pedophile apologist

OK, let's break that down:

"This has struck a kind of tribal nerve in Catholicism."

Oh, a tribal nerve . . . well, that's good. Heaven forbid people make policy based on a rational response to a problem—go with the caveman thinking. This "tribal nerve"—is that the same instinctual feeling that kept the previous Pope from turning in any of the molesters on his payroll?

"The Catholic Church has been beaten up for the last ten or eleven years . . ."

Hey world, why do you keep beating up on the Catholics? Oh, right, the molesting and the covering up . . . . Still, can we all quit bullying one of the most powerful institutions in the world that refuses to take responsibility for one of the largest criminal conspiracies in history?

"Catholics are tired of the government and others beating up on the church. . . ."

Oh, yes, how the government beats up on the church, with their appropriate criminal investigations. And can you believe the government with their letting you keep your non-profit status, even though you frequently make political recommendations to your parishioners? I don't know how you Catholics carry on.

Can you believe it? The people who brought you the Inquisition, suppressed the science of Galileo and Darwin, turned a blind eye during the Holocaust, and molested children—I mean, can you believe we are making them provide diaphragms to women who want to have sex?!

So the Catholic Church thinks it's a victim? I really would suggest they talk to a few actual victims—like those of molestation or homophobia—and get a more empirical understanding of what victimhood is.

FAITH TRUMPS REASON

"Donald Trump, when I first saw that he was getting in, I thought, 'Well this has got to be a joke,' but the more you listen to him, the more you say to yourself, 'You know, maybe the guy's right.'"
—Billy Graham's son

This is a video clip to keep—everyone should put it on their hard drive, then back up that hard drive. Because this is the clip you pull out every time Franklin Graham tries to say anything credible ever again. It's over, Franklin—you officially gave up any claims you might have had on rational thought. Supporting Donald Trump?! I would have to say that's worse than actually being Donald Trump.

I mean, "the Donald" has an excuse—he's a full-blown lunatic who has to live in the head of a full-blown lunatic. And everyone can see that—he has an entire television show dedicated to the fact that he's a deluded, self-important megalomaniac. But you, Franklin Graham, you as an objective observer, who has watched and listened to Donald Trump all these years; you ultimately said to yourself, "Yeah, that's my guy—that's the horse I'm betting on"?

I'm sorry, but as an atheist, I look at all religious leaders as suspect at best. And I gotta say, Frank, you've managed to make pretty much everyone else look good with a single endorsement. You know the Pope that condemned Galileo? He just moved up a notch in my book. The crack-head-slash-preacher at my grocery store just moved up in the rankings—cuz Frank, you said that the more you listen to Donald Trump, the more you think he's right about stuff.

Yeah, I get it now. You mean, the more you listen to Donald Trump's nonstop cowardly innuendo, shameless race baiting, and xenophobia . . . after hearing that for awhile, you say to yourself, "Maybe this guy's right!"

Franklin Graham, I hope to God you never come up with the cure for cancer—cuz there's no way anybody is going to believe you.

CARDINAL SIN

"It's part of our religion, it's part of our faith that we feed the hungry, that we educate the kids, that we take care of the sick. . . . We have to give it up because we are unable to fit the description and the definition of a church, given by . . . the federal government."
—Cardinal Dolan, explaining God's opposition to Obamacare

Well, it's been a little while since we've heard from the Keystone Cops of morality—the Catholic Church. But not to worry, just like a case of herpes given to you by a priest, they always come back.

(Background info: The federal government gives Catholic charities $2.9 billion a year for their charity work; keep that in mind as you read this chapter.)

Sooo . . . the healthcare reform law (Obamacare) stipulates that providers must offer birth control. Which is totally reasonable, unless you believe sperm is a magical elixir and human ova are tiny little Eucharist—like the Catholic Church does.

Although the church itself does not have to provide such healthcare to its employees, its secular institutions, like Catholic hospitals and schools, must provide this type of insurance. I know, can you believe it? Some liberal Jewish lady working in accounting at St. Jude's Hospital wants the pill? What a jezebel.

So, someone at MSNBC thought it would be a good idea to point a microphone at the Timothy Dolan, Cardinal of New York (in Latin, "Cardinal" means cover-up).

> **"When these mandates click in, we're going to find ourselves faced with a terribly difficult decision as to whether or not we can continue to operate. It's part of our religion, it's part of our faith that we feed the hungry, that we educate the kids, that we take care of the sick. . . .**
>
> **"We have to give it up because we are unable to fit the description and the definition of a church, given by . . . the federal government."**

I had trouble following that logic, too—what with it being illogical and all. What the Cardinal is saying is, if they are required to offer birth control to its lay employees, it would be so immoral, they would have to shut down all those institutions—because the federal government is under some crazy delusion that a hospital is not a church, a school isn't a church.

Isn't that crazy? What he's saying is: God wants us to do good works, but not if it means a tiny percentage of the insurance we provide to our employees might stop one sperm from meeting one egg. That, sir, is a bridge too far.

So let me get this straight, God commands you to serve the poor, the sick, and the needy, and the government even gives you a couple billion dollars to help you do just that, but you're not gonna do it because the idea of contraception is so sinful to you that it makes you wanna turn your back on the poor and needy? Or did God tell you that, if Obamacare passes, forget about that "help the poor" bullshit?

I wonder if he consulted the poor and sick children that will be affected by his decision, or if he just consulted with the usual group of criminal child-rapist-protectors and closeted homosexuals that we usually hear from. I hear the pedophiles and those in the church that harbor them are on board with making them even more desperate and easy to exploit.

So to sum up, yes, this guy is that much of a maniac about sex that he would rather turn his back on starving children than give women access to family planning.

Can you believe everyone is making a thing out of this? Cardinal Dolan can't:

"We don't want this fight, my Lord, we just want to be left alone to the work that we feel Jesus asked us to do."
—Cardinal Dolan

Oh really, you want the government to leave you alone? You mean after you collect the $2.9 billion or before? And let me get this straight, *you are still gonna collect the charity money, you just aren't going to disperse it?*

I, for one, would love to leave the Catholic Church alone to do the work Jesus commanded them to do—like molesting children, teaching shame of the human body, and demonizing homosexuals. However, there's always that little problem that Catholic institutions employ thousands of people who have basic rights and privileges under the law.

Cardinal Dolan, I got it! You won't have to worry about this law if, from now on, your schools and hospitals only employ strict Catholics who think a diaphragm is Satan's beanie! That's totally feasible, right? What with all those qualified workers out there that still believe the completely reasonable dogmas of the Catholic Church . . . right?

And by the way, and this isn't funny, but Cardinal Dolan just summed up everything that is wrong with the Catholic Church.

They just want to be left alone. In other words, as always, they don't want to be part of the time and place in which they are operating. They want the MRI machine in their hospital, but they want to ignore the diagnostic manual that says homosexuality isn't a disease.

You know that once in awhile, if not frequently, Cardinal Dolan thinks, "It was so much easier when the church ran all of Europe and no one told us what to do . . . what was that called again? Oh yeah, 'The Dark Ages.'"

I'M GOING TO HELL!

I find that people who need to be publicly religious are always putting on a show of one form or another, and I am always suspect of them. All the mainstream religious "group thinks," and that scale scares me. You don't get to think your own thoughts about things inside religions.

Oh sure, I hear the religious now, "No, no, no, we *encourage* questions!"

Oh really? You encourage *questions*? But you only *encourage* one answer, correct?

What if your answers aren't the ones the church has to those questions? I mean, you can't start coming up with your own answers to questions that contradict church doctrine and still stay in the church, can you?

Why do religious people get a pass for being ignorant in ways other people don't? For instance, if I think that gays are defective, immoral, and will burn in hell, then I'm just a good Christian. Or just a good Muslim, or a good Jew. Why is it that the more religious you are, the more ignorant you are allowed to be in America?

In our society, there is the expectation that we should watch what we say around the overly religious. Some members of my family are waaaaaay too religious—like the "born again" kind of crazy. Last year, I was at a family reunion with my parents and a few of my brothers, sitting around a picnic table having some laughs and talking about the latest, craziest thing Pat Robertson had said when some "born agains" pulled up in their car.

"Hey, watch what you say about religion, here comes Angela and her family, and they are really sensitive about that stuff," my father immediately warned us.

And we all quickly changed the subject as to not offend this overly religious family member. And it pissed me off, I mean, 'til this day it pisses me off that I let that happen and didn't say something.

Why? Because I am sick of politely dancing around the people who claim to be saved and know they are going to heaven. If you are so sure and so filled with God's love, then what in the world could anything I say ever mess you up?

Thinking you are going to heaven, forever, eternity, everlasting life with Jesus, in just a few short years . . . but you can't stand being in the presence of a little public secular reasoning? Really? Then I guess you aren't really all that sure of yourself. Sounds to me like you aren't standing on too solid of ground if you can be thrown into a tizzy by anyone expressing their own disbelief.

I wanted to tell my dad, "Hey pop, you know how I'm an atheist? How about if you ask those religious crazies to swallow all their Jesus talk when they are around me, cuz you know how sensitive I am about it."

See what I mean? Turning the tables, why aren't knee-jerk reactions to atheists filled with the same kind of reverence for my ideas and the same kind of concern for my easily hurt feelings? Why are atheists not allowed to have sensitive feelings about our beliefs? Why is it that the woman who is super sure that she's going to heaven and so sure that I'm going to hell gets to scream it at me? Why is it that she gets to play the victim instead of the bully that she is?

I think it's because those people secretly don't believe their own bullshit. Anything that undermines the fundamentalist fairy tale they are living in is "offensive and insulting." Because they secretly doubt it, too, and when you give voice to those doubts, they have to shut that shit up, and quick.

I'll never forget the time I was on stage in Cleveland, and I was doing my usual jokes about growing up Catholic with 11 siblings:

> **"I grew up Catholic, but I was never that into it. My par-
> ents, on the other hand, were reeeeally Catholic. I mean
> reeeeally Catholic, like they almost molested somebody. . . .
> I'm talking hardcore Catholics. . . . I was more of a 'buffet
> Catholic,' I didn't follow all the dogma, only took what I
> liked—a little sin forgiveness without judgment, and some
> unconditional love . . . but I'll skip the molestation and
> subjugation of women parts."**

At that point I heard a noise. It was a woman very loudly putting her coat on. I don't know how you put a coat on loudly, but believe me, she did it.

As she walked out and I asked "What happened? Was it something I said?" and she responded at the top of her lungs, "YOU'RE GOING TO HELL!" You know, just like Jesus would say.

And it struck me at that moment that she didn't really think I was going to hell. She was *wishing* that I were going to hell. In my mind, if she really did think I was going to hell when I died . . . wouldn't she be nicer to me now???

Does she always take so much satisfaction in delivering such horrible news to strangers? Does she run up to smokers the same way? Does she get in their face and scream gleefully, "YOU'RE GONNA GET CANCER!! HA HA!"?

If she really and truly thought I was going to hell and was going to burn in hell for making a couple of jokes about religion, don't you think her response would be concern?

Her outburst wasn't concern for my soul or pity for my eternity of burning in a lake of fire. As I learned from Oprah, anger almost always masks another emotion, and that emotion is fear.

She was not angry that what I was saying was wrong and blasphemous; my comedy was agitating that part of her brain that is worried that her whole life might actually be a fraud. Unlike this woman, who has internalized other people's thoughts and ideas on spirituality and the meaning of life, I was giving myself the permission to not only think contrary thoughts about religion, but I was also giving myself permission to say those things publicly without fear of repercussions.

Those feeling a need to publicly shout down people expressing disbelief in a higher power, or for ridiculing religion, is a manifestation of their own internal doubt about their own beliefs, and they are unable to shout them down inside their own heads, and so do it externally.

So those that do that are really immature, un-evolved, emotional children who are too scared to actually confront their own inner doubts, so they become outer assholes in a very loud, dysfunctional way.

That's my theory, anyway. And if you don't like it, then tell me to go to hell. Just don't do it in the middle of my stand-up show.

WHAT ELSE
IS
WRONG?

TORTUROUS

"The healthy man does not torture others—it is the tortured who turn into torturers."
    –Carl Jung

"I was a big supporter of waterboarding."
    –Dick Cheney

So America tortures now, and nobody seems to care. Oh, we don't call it torture. Calling it torture makes us feel icky, like we're a bunch of torturers or something. No, torture is wrong; what we do is called "enhanced interrogation techniques." Which sounds nice, doesn't it? Enhanced interrogation techniques.

"Oh it's enhanced? . . . Are you going to put on some mood music and a little track lighting?"

"No, we're going to hook your balls up to a car battery and then drown you."

"Oh, I'll just take the regular interrogation then, don't make a fuss over me."

The people who ordered torture say it really works! In fact, it works so well they waterboarded one guy 183 times. Now if it really works so well, why do you have to repeatedly waterboard this guy? Wouldn't he give up all his info in the first few torture sessions? What are the questions you are still asking on the 183rd waterboard?

"Do these pants make me look fat? Have you seen my keys?"

Yeah, so we illegally invaded another country, killed a bunch of their people, tortured a bunch more, and nobody goes to jail. Not that the government doesn't like putting people in jail in America

. . . We love it! In fact, the United States leads the world in locking up its own citizens. We lock up even more people than China. America is Number One! Suck it.

But we don't lock up all the citizens. For instance, not the rich white guys who invade countries illegally and order war crimes. No, those guys get a pass, but a poor black kid with a roach in his pocket gets the full force of the law.

Just to blow your mind for a minute before I get back to torture, think about this:

Approximately half of all drug arrests are for marijuana. That's one marijuana arrest every 42 seconds for something most Americans don't think should even be a crime.

The Louisiana Supreme Court overturned a sentence of five years because they considered it too lenient for a fourth possession of marijuana. They ordered the person to a sentence of 13 years. In Louisiana, you could get up to six months in jail for your first marijuana conviction, up to five years for a second conviction, and up to twenty years in prison for a third. If you ask me, that doesn't seem like the Mardi Gras spirit.

So it's not a war on drugs or crime, but a war on the American people. Okay, keep that in mind, now back to torture.

Barack Obama gave the order to not prosecute any of the people involved with ordering or carrying out those war crimes. The president rationalized not prosecuting them by saying all those crimes happened in the past, and President Obama is looking toward the future!

When I heard that, I felt a lot better. Because all the crimes I've committed are in the past, too. Glad we aren't prosecuting those anymore! I bet all those people in prison are pissed off they committed their crimes in the future. Stupid criminals.

So what is my point? I guess my point is that I can't figure out why everyone isn't screaming at the top of their lungs every day about this shit.

It is now official American policy to turn a blind eye to the worst crimes possible, but hammer the poor for next to nothing. Yes, America would rather put you in jail for "mellowing out" than for lying your nation into an illegal invasion and ordering war crimes. Your country is just not that into you!

SPIES LIKE US

 "The way in which the NSA is spying on American citizens is in violation of the Fourth Amendment of the United States Constitution, as well as in excess of the limitations imposed by the statute, the FISA Amendments Act of 2008. In other words, what the NSA is doing is both unconstitutional and illegal."
—Glenn Greenwald, actual journalist

So the American people are being spied on by their own government.

Turns out they are tapping our phones and reading our emails without a warrant.

And that's not a big deal unless . . . well, unless you read the Constitution, and who has time for that? I'm not an egghead or something.

But I do know some people who have read the Constitution, and they say that the government tapping our phones and reading our emails . . . is pretty fucked up.

And why are they doing this? Well, because the government says the terrorists hate our freedom, and they want to take it!

So to fight those terrorists, the government is gonna take our freedom first!

That'll show those Al Qaeda bastards. Oh, how I'd like to see the look on their stupid-terrorist-faces when they get here. I can hear them now:

Terrorist: "Where is your freedom that I hate?!"

Me: "Got rid of it . . . *psyche*!!!"

So just to re-cap, the government is taking our freedoms in order to preserve our freedoms. Wow, you know what they say about that, right? Well, they say that when "fascism" comes to America it will look like "antifascism."

And you know what I say? I say, "What does *fascism* mean?"

It's the biggest story of government lying and breaking the law since Watergate and the Pentagon papers.

Now the person who brought all of this to our attention is whistle-blower Edward Snowden, who worked for a private contractor doing work for the National Security Agency. He then sold it to Russia and China for millions of dollars cuz he is a horrible traitor.

Oh wait, that's not what he did, that is just how they make it seem like in the media. What he actually did was pass that information to a responsible journalist at a responsible newspaper, Glenn Greenwald at the *Guardian*, and ask him to reveal what he thought was vital for the American people to know.

Snowden's an old-fashioned kinda guy. He didn't post the information willy nilly on a website, or sell it to a foreign power for huge sums of money. No, he gave the information about illegal activity to a news organization, exactly what a responsible citizen should do, in the same manner that important past whistleblowers like Daniel Ellsberg and Deep Throat did.

So Glenn Greenwald goes on *Meet the Press* to tell us all about it, but what ended up happening was a lesson in bad journalism via David "Mr. Handsome Say Stuff To Camera" Gregory.

Having invited an actual journalist on his show, a journalist who actually broke a huge story of illegality inside the government, and David immediately sensed something was wrong . . .

"To the extent that you have aided and abetted Snowden, even in his current movements, why shouldn't you, Mr. Greenwald, be charged with a crime?"
  —David Gregory, shitty journalist

Yes, David thinks he oughta be put in jail for his efforts. Of course, that's why Gregory never does any real journalism . . . he thinks it's illegal!

Greenwald then gives one of the all-time dressing-downs I have ever seen on television.

"I think it's pretty extraordinary that anyone who would call themselves a journalist would publicly muse about whether or not other journalists should be charged with felonies. The assumption in your question David is completely without evidence, the idea that I've aided and abetted him in any way.

"The scandal that arose in Washington before our stories began was about the fact that the Obama administration is trying to criminalize investigative journalism, by going through the emails and phone records of AP journalists, accusing a Fox News journalist of the theory that you just embraced—being a co-conspirator in felonies for working with sources.

"If you want to embrace that theory, that means that every investigative journalist in the United States that works with their sources, who receives classified information, is a criminal. And it is precisely those theories and precisely that climate that has become so menacing in the United States; it's why in the New Yorker, Jane Mayer said that *investigative* journalism has ground to a standstill."
  —Glenn Greenwald

Okay, Mr. Greenwald, isn't that all a fancy way of saying you admire a guy who gave up a six-figure job and cushy life in Hawaii to announce that the government lies about shit?

So after getting his ass handed to him for furthering government talking points, Gregory responds with:

"Well the question of 'who is a journalist' may be up to a debate in regards to what you are doing. Anybody who is watching this understands I was asking a question, that question has been raised by lawmakers as well; I'm not embracing anything."

Yeah, the question of "who's a journalist" is definitely up for debate, especially on your show. And you weren't embracing bullshit government talking points, you were just repeating them on your show in the first person *instead of debunking them*! Now back to that "who's a fucking journalist" debate . . .

The ridiculous question of whether his investigative journalism should land him in jail kind of pissed Greenwald off, and after the show he tweeted:

"Who needs the government to try and criminalize journalism when you have David Gregory around?"

To which Captain Corporate Tool responded:

"This is the problem from somebody who claims that he's a journalist, who would object to a journalist raising questions, which is not actually embracing any particular point of view. . . . rather than going after the questioner, he could take on the issues."

Funny how Gregory can ask the guy doing real journalism if he should go to jail for it, but when Greenwald questions your "journalism," you whine that he's shooting the messenger. It's about time network journalists started cracking down on actual journalists.

TAKE A PEW

After denying that the government was spying on its citizens, Obama recently made promises to reform the NSA's data collecting. As this book goes to print, the details are hazy, but the gist is that instead of the government bulk collecting your phone data, the phone companies will do it for them. This will free up time for the NSA to read your emails. It's amazing we got to this point, because looking at PEW polling data after Snowden's revelations, the public didn't seem very bothered.

Turns out YOU just aren't that into you either.

Perceptions of the Government's Data Collection Program

Do courts provide adequate limits on what is collected?

Yes	No	DK
30	56	15

Is the government using this data. . .

Only for anti-terror	Also for other purposes	DK
22	70	7

Is the government collecting. . .

Only meta data	Also what is being said in phone calls and emails	DK
18	63	18

Has the government listened to YOUR calls or read YOUR emails?

Yes	No	DK
27	28	8

PEW RESEARCH CENTER July 17-21, 2013
figures may not add to 100% due to rounding

So it's interesting that most people *don't* believe the government when they say they *are not* listening to our calls or reading our emails.

AND YET:

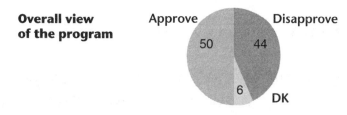

Overall view of the program   Approve   Disapprove   50   44   6   DK

PEW RESEARCH CENTER July 17-21, 2013
figures may not add to 100% due to rounding

YES! Half the people are still cool with it!!!!

WTF?

Imagine how shitty the Constitution would be if they had to write it today?

So 70% think the government is violating our Constitutional rights, but maybe that's one of their Constitutional rights.

So I guess what most people are thinking is that, "Yes, we know the NSA is completely full of shit . . . but they must have a perfectly good reason!"

It's like an abusive relationship. Sure, the government's lying to us, but deep down we deserve it.

That's what's great about having a Bill of Rights—you don't have to use any of them if you don't feel like it.

MEET MY META

"You listen to a lot of the coverage, and you would think we had literally millions and millions of FBI agents listening to every single call that every single American makes; that simply is not true. And I think having this

conversation with the American people is an important thing to do."

—Robert Gibbs, previous White House spokesman, lying about spying

So, the White House thinks having that discussion with the American people is an important thing to do? Too bad you weren't for having it before Edward Snowden blew the whistle on you guys. Weird how that works.

Our grandparents had NASA—we got NSA. Princeton computer science professor Edward Felten has written about why the government collecting its citizens' metadata is so invasive. The more metadata you collect, the more powerful it becomes.

For example, let's imagine that metadata reveals a call to an illegal bookie; now the NSA knows that a person made an illegal bet with that bookie. And what's more, "analysis of metadata over time could reveal that the target has a gambling problem, particularly if the call records also reveal a number of calls made to payday loan services."

"Consider the following hypothetical example: A young woman calls her gynecologist; then immediately calls her mother; then a man who, during the past few months, she had repeatedly spoken to on the telephone after 11pm; followed by a call to a family planning center that also offers abortions. A likely storyline emerges that would not be as evident by examining the record of a single telephone call."

The storyline is that she's easy, and now the government knows it.

So this is how the government, by knowing *who* you're calling, gathers information that violates our privacy. And to all those people saying, "It's just metadata," I say, "You're a porn addict, your son harasses girls on Facebook, and your wife is cheating on you."

By the way, do you know who else consistently uses this kind of data? Private industry. This is why the private contractors involved in the data gathering scare me silly. Let's say there's a land developer who wants to drive out a bunch of residents in a particular area. Imagine he had access to the e-mails and call records of those residents. Now imagine that private information getting easily exploited because the firewall of security around that data has been extinguished, thanks to the water hose of clearances given to private companies.

You don't have to imagine the last part because it's true. I hear some people respond that those thousands of private contractors wouldn't have been given high security clearance if they were apt to leak that information . . . except that Edward Snowden was one of those people, and he did. Even though he did it for good reasons, what's to stop Joe Nitwit with gambling debts from doing the same thing, only this time with something we do want secret and to someone we'd rather not have those secrets.

In the years after 9/11, the world of intelligence grew like mold. The NSA and CIA hired of outside firms to help gather and analyze data. Among the many reasons why this is a problem is the inefficiency. There is a high rate of redundancy in the system and far too many cooks in the kitchen. With this, we get worrying situations where the company Snowden worked for, Booz Allen Hamilton, is owned by the Carlyle Group, an investment company with strong ties to Saudi Arabian oligarchs. However, it was the Republican wet dream

- Privatizing a traditionally public trust? How could that possibly go wrong?
- Introducing a hefty profit motive into threat assessment? There's no way that could lead us down a garden path.

· Giving multi-national corporations with various business interests access to the entire world's private communications. Perfect!

This expansion has created a huge multi-headed beast which of course will seek to perpetuate itself while ignoring any and all fiduciary duties it might have to the public. Of course, this beast sought to grow in power and scope, if only to consolidate its own power.

One of the many side-effects of this growing beast was an explosion in the number and speed of Top Secret or higher clearances issued. Which is clearly dangerous.

The more people know a secret, the less likely it'll remain a secret. Whether you believe in these programs or not, this represents sheer recklessness on the part of policy-makers, for the sake of giving private industry a piece of the action. "We're trying to gather and keep secrets, and we're pretty sure the best way to do that is by telling these secrets to 300% more people."

Edward Snowden is a hero. There is no doubt about that. We should all be grateful that Snowden had access to this information, and at great risk to himself, exposed these programs to the American public. But I can be grateful to Snowden, while at the same time recognizing that his access to this information is, itself, problematic. Maybe that's a paradox, but I'll happily live with the headache of trying to sort it out.

CAN YOU KEEP A SECRET?

"A secretive U.S. Drug Enforcement Administration unit is funneling information from [NSA] intelligence intercepts, wiretaps, informants and a massive database of telephone records to authorities across the nation to help them launch criminal investigations of Americans . . ."
—Reuters

So it's way worse than anyone thought. They are lying at every step. They are listening to your calls, they are collecting your data, and if they find anything illegal at all, even if it has ZERO to do with terrorism, they will alert local law enforcement. Feel safer?

But come on, everybody knows you can't make an omelet without violating the Constitution.

I know it sounds bad, but if you don't give cops the tools they need to fight crime, they'll have to go back to planting drugs on people.

Although it got very little attention in the mainstream press when it was reported, Reuters did, in fact, report that tips derived from NSA surveillance are being provided to domestic law enforcement for lots of non-terrorist crimes, like selling pot to your friends. It's worth reading that again:

"A secretive [DEA] unit is funneling information from [NSA] intelligence intercepts . . . to authorities across the nation to help them launch criminal investigations of Americans."
—Reuters

I have to keep repeating this information because I can hardly believe it myself.

This is the part of the *Law and Order* episode when the judge throws out the evidence because it arose from an illegal search. And then the lesser character actor playing the defense attorney says, "Mr. McCoy wants to go on a fishing expedition!" Unfortunately for us, this is the part where it turns out there is a bigger conspiracy to subvert the law, usually led by someone who had a film career in the late eighties—let's say it's Rick Moranis in this week's episode.

Here's the deal: No agent of law enforcement can execute any search or surveillance of a person who has a reasonable expectation of privacy. So, for instance, if you hear your neighbor through the wall conspiring to steal cable, you can go and tell the police, and they can use that information to obtain a warrant to build a case. Now, to be fair, if you did this, you'd be a total narc, and no one will sit with you at lunch, and you'd better get used to being a virgin, you tattletale.

On the other hand, an agent of any intelligence or police agency that got that Information—that's a no-no. Even if the local dog catcher happened to be using a parabolic microphone to sweep your building because he's a total perv, this information is not usable by the Cable Police (yeah, sure, that's a thing).

What's even worse here is a criminal conspiracy to subvert the law. It would be like Briscoe and Logan illegally obtained information, then told the SVU detectives about it, but said it should sound like it came from a unnamed confidential informant. Then Ice-T comes in and gives some piece of information, and you're all like, "How the fuck does that guy have a job as an actor, because seriously . . . "

So your worst fears about government spying are true, they are listening in on your phone conversations and then ILLEGALLY using that info to prosecute you for regular, everyday "run-of-the-mill" crimes that nobody should care about unless you run in mills.

Could it get worse? Yes, it's the government, it always gets worse.

After the NSA provides the information to the DEA who then provides it to local law enforcement, they are then instructed to scrub where they got the evidence from. Agents are instructed to then use "normal investigative techniques to recreate the information provided by the Special Operations Division."

So, just to review: Illegally obtained information which, because of its illegality, cannot be used as evidence later, nor can any other evidence which may arise from this information. AND a massive 100% criminal conspiracy on the part of the CIA, NSA, FBI, DEA, DHS, SOD, HBO etc. . . . to subvert the Fourth Amendment. Got it?

You're not paranoid, they really are out to get you—and they're bad at it, too.

But that's what really makes this the greatest country in the world; they don't tell us they're violating our civil liberties.

And remember, it's not like we're China . . . we have *two* political parties spying on us.

GUNS 'R' US

So the Dems are gonna try and regulate guns, but they really love guns, really. God forbid there is a person who wants to regulate guns that actually hates them. Here is Harry Reid giving his "I love guns" speech, but it gets a little weird:

"I had guns from the time I was a little boy . . . I keep them for sentimental reasons. My dad killed himself, shot himself with a gun, committed suicide, so I know a lot about guns."
—Harry Reid

Um, Harry, is there a better story to illustrate why you love guns than the one where your dad uses one to kill himself? Cuz that seems a little fucked up . . . . "See that bottle of Celebrex? My uncle was killed by a stroke caused by Vioxx, so I keep that bottle around, kind of sentimental about it."

Seriously, where are you going with this, Harry? Cuz I'm starting to think this is just you waxing poetic about guns.

In about ten seconds, this is going to turn into scene from *Spinal Tap*, and Nigel Tufnel is gonna take a guitar tour of Harry Reid's awesome gun collection. "On this one, if you listen closely, you can still hear the bang from when my dad blew his head off. And this gun goes to eleven . . ."

BANG! BANG! YOU'RE DEAD INSIDE

Newt Gingrich says secularism led to mass shooting. Media reacts by having him as respected guest on every TV news show.

Tennessee considers training its teachers to use guns in classrooms. They have yet to train teachers to use books in classrooms.

 "We ask, 'Why there is violence in our schools?' when we've systematically removed God from our schools."
—Mike Huckabee immediately after the Newtown massacre of 20 children ages 6 and 7 with a rifle.

"Where was God? God is not going to go where he is not wanted . . . we've kicked God out of our schools . . ."
—Bryan Fischer, host of *Focal Point*, another religious asshole

Pesky God, always needs to be *ASKED* to save 6-year-olds from getting slaughtered. Does *God* ever take the initiative on something like this? Cuz it seems like he should, even if it's breaking a rule or something, don't you think?

I mean if God intervenes on math tests and puppy rescues, maybe he sticks his chin out and protects some kids from a nutcase with a rifle?

And no matter how many times these people have to be told that what they are saying is stupid and offensive, it just doesn't seem to sink in. And no matter how many times you tell them about separation of church and state, they still think that, in a secular society, the place to teach God is public school.

Here is a grown man who was governor of a state, and he thinks 20 kids got blown away cuz God got mad. Maybe he thinks it was God's way to show us that we should have put "under God" in the Pledge of Allegiance . . . wait, we did!

Mike Huckabee asks, "Why did God let this happen?" and his answer is that God really hates when you stop talking about him. And since Huckabee is dead set against gun control laws, we all better start praying.

> **"If we are going to change things, it is going to take a wave of Americans . . . standing up saying 'enough' on behalf of our kids."**
> **—Barack Obama takes tough stand on overwhelmingly popular gun bill**

Yes, it is going to take a stream of Americans because we've got a steady stream of gutless politicians who cower in fear of the NRA.

Right, that's how you change things, you wait until EVERYBODY IN THE WHOLE WIDE WORLD thinks the same way, then we try and pass sensible gun legislation.

What is it going to take to pass gun legislation?

> **"It will take commitment and compromise, and most of all it will take courage."**
> **—Prez Obama**

Great, so that assures it won't get done.

> **"I'm not so sure I wouldn't want one person in a school armed and ready for this kind of thing."**
> **—William Bennett, degenerate gambler and author of**
> ***The Book of Virtues.***

Seriously, how much longer can we tolerate elementary schools without their own militia?

To Bill Bennett, the lesson of Newtown is that we need more principals and school psychologists packing heat. And the school nurse should carry a hunting knife.

And of course, he's all for doing whatever we can to prevent this kind of tragedy from happening again, except for changing gun laws.

YOUR RIGHT TO WORK . . .
AT WAL-MART WAGES

> **"Right to work . . . is about being pro-workers, giving workers the choice; if anything, this should encourage unions to be more responsive to workers."**
> **—Rick Snyder, Governor of Michigan, speaking with**
> **a straight face**

Yeah, right to work gives the workers a choice . . . take it or leave it.

I don't know how close you are following Michigan, but they passed anti-union legislation, aka "Right to Work," and check out the governor, Mr. Straight Face over here:

> **"It's about economic development. We will get more and better jobs coming to Michigan, because we're going to be more competitive."**
> **—Gov. Snyder, again straight-facing it**

Michigan will get all kinds of jobs, like they have in China, and for the same wages. Anyway, it'll all work out because, once the unions are crushed, nobody will ever have to pay dues ever again.

Hey, come on, let's be realistic, does everybody need a living wage, really?

The Republicans don't hate the workers . . . they're just nostalgic for labor conditions during the Taft administration. And what nobody's mentioned is, this law goes a long way toward protecting the rights of scabs.

LABORED

Okay, it's fun to watch Gov. Snyder straight-face his laughable lie about helping workers, but what is the real reason Republicans kill unions?

> **"You keep having a half a million people leave the labor movement every year, and pretty soon you start having a crimp in the political budgets of these unions; it has a direct effect on the presidential race."**
> **—Karl Rove, revealing the real reason for "right to work" legislation—to accumulate political power**

So you're saying that "more and better jobs" horseshit was just a political smokescreen? Okay, just checking. A power grab that lowers the wages of working people. Hmm, I wonder why you guys are worried you don't connect with the public more.

At that same moment, thousands of supporters showed up outside the Michigan State Capitol to protest the stripping of union rights. Steve Crowder, an ass-hat "investigative reporter" for Fox News, sees a chance to get some action-packed video, so he starts to get in the face of protesters. One of the protesters described him as "a guy who wasn't going home until he got punched." And guess what? The instigative reporter eventually got punched, much to his delight. An edited video made the rounds, and the creepy Crowder unsuccessfully tried to act like a naïve innocent.

Then we move on to *Morning Joe*, and he is baffled at why a union member would take a swing at a mouthpiece for the plutocrats in the middle of an all-out assault on working families:

> **"I don't understand the video at all. That doesn't justify people punching people because they feel threatened economically. If conservatives go around punching people like that, it would've been the lead on every newscast in America, I just worry about the double standard."**
> **—Joe Scarborough**

Nothing outrages Joe Scarborough more than the suffering of another white man.

When is somebody going to stand up for a conservative's right to crush labor unions?

Can you believe those union thugs—when their job security's taken away, they actually get pissed off about it?

If a liberal had gotten punched, it would've been the lead in every news story in the country—you mean like how this one was the lead on your news story? Or like when that woman was beaten up at the Rand Paul rally and got her head stomped? OK, bad example.

My question is, why did it take so long to start punching reporters from Fox News?

On the other hand, Joe Scarborough practically begs to get punched in the face every morning, and it never happens once.

"If conservatives go around punching people like that, it would've been the lead on every newscast in America; I just worry about the double standard."

Oh PLEASE, does he mean a DOUBLE STANDARD that doesn't work in rich guys' favor in America?

Cops brutalized Occupy Wall Street protesters, maced pregnant women, students, and senior citizens, yet we heard none of this same outrage from Joe.

Suck a dick with your self-pity for the party of the put-upon white man. Oh, the media is so biased against conservatives that, if I don't agree with conservative republican Joe Scarborough, I have the option of turning on the liberal morning talk show that doesn't exist.

Once again, Scarborough displays the moral courage needed to stand up for the wealthy and powerful.

"What is wrong with the state allowing an American to work wherever he wants to work without being compelled to pay union dues?"
—Joe Scarborough

Because it spells the END of unions and FOR COLLECTIVE BARGAINING RIGHTS of workers.

If we don't have collective bargaining, then we have everybody working at Wal-Mart and McDonald's wages, and our economy goes in the shitter because money is now concentrated in fewer hands, which slows down the economy.

A study by economist Lonnie K. Stevans of Hofstra University found that states that have enacted such laws reported no increase in business start-ups or rates of employment. Wages and personal income are lower in those states than in those without such laws, though the proprietor incomes are higher; in short, right-to-work laws simply redistribute income from the workers to the owners.

We keep treating these problems like they are individual problems, when they are societal problems.

> **"Am I anti-union for saying, 'I should be able to work where I want to work and pay union dues if I want to pay union dues,' is that an anti-union position or is it just supporting freedom?"**
> **—Joe "Holy Shit" Scarborough**

In response to Scarborough's simulated outrage, Harold Ford springs into action with apologetic mumbling and then says:

> **"I think it's supporting freedom."**

Fearing retribution from Boss Man Scarborough, Harold Ford folds like a lawn chair. Maybe if there was a union for talk show guests, he could've spoken his mind.

MEDICARE MEDDLING

> **"We can play the political game, or we can actually be absolutely honest with the American people on Medicare."**
> **—Senator Tom Coburn, Washington game player, right before lying about Medicare**

I've learned that whenever somebody says, "I'm not a racist, but . . ." that it is a sign that I should get ready for some racist shit right away. Same thing when someone feels the need to say, "to be honest." When I hear that, I get ready for a stream of heartfelt, overly sincere, complete bullshit. If he were going to be honest, he would say that he's getting ready to screw poor and middle class people again while continuing to give government handouts to his corporate overlords.

Whenever someone says Medicare is going bankrupt (or anything in the government is going bankrupt), that's how you know they are full of shit. Medicare, like all government programs, doesn't go bankrupt; we either choose to fund them or we don't choose to fund them, period.

It's funny how only the programs that actually work and help people are the ones always going bankrupt. Why doesn't anyone ever talk about how the Pentagon is going bankrupt? Are they still turning a profit over at the Pentagon? Afghan war still in the black, is it?

Another surefire way a politician is full of shit is if he proposes to fix a problem that isn't going to happen for 25 years. Social Security is solvent until 2037, and with very minor fixes is solvent until 2080. I have never heard of a politician wanting to solve a problem that isn't going to happen until he's long gone from office and even dead.

So when a politician says, "We have to fix Social Security from going bankrupt," ask him what other problems that won't happen for 25 years does he think we need to fix right now? I've never heard of a politician wanting to fix a problem that is 25 years out.

And let's remember the problem with Medicare is the problem with healthcare; our healthcare costs are twice as high as those of the rest of the industrialized world. Medicare costs aren't driving up healthcare costs; *healthcare costs are driving up our Medicare costs.* So you can't fix Medicare without fixing healthcare costs, which nobody has any interest in doing.

One of my favorite things is when a real phony asshole tells us we have to "shoot straight" and then blatantly lies. A comedic rule of thumb is "lying is always funny," and for my money, there are few "funnier" than Tom Coburn.

Not only does he tell us that he's gonna shoot straight and then blatantly lie, but he goes the extra mile and uses Orwellian language to cover up what he is really planning on doing, as witnessed in his use of the term "individual participation" in the following quote.

> **"We have to stop playing the game; you can't continue to lie to the American people. . . . The way to fix [Medicare] is to control the cost, and the way to control the cost is to have more individual participation . . . and yes, everybody in this country will have to participate in some discomfort if we are to get out of this mess."**
> **—Senator Tom Coburn, selling bullshit as a "harsh truth"**

Let me explain: "Individual participation" is a technical term which means "elderly people get to choose between food or medicine." It means that old people with no income have to pay more out of their already empty pockets. That's what "increased participation" means; it means old people *participate* in *paying more.*

But don't worry, because as the overly earnest-sounding senator just told us, everybody will have to participate in some discomfort—except, of course, for the people who don't really need Medicare.

In 2011 alone, out-of-pocket medical expenses pushed over 10 million people into poverty, and the senior poverty rate would be cut in half if not for their out-of-pocket medical expenses.

And Senator Tom "Straight Shooter" Coburn's solution is to make those senior citizens pay more! That's just common sense; if we're going to get out of this hole, we're going to have to throw a lot of poor people into it. Or to put it another way, we are going to have to re-adjust the safety net so it has a hole big enough for all the poor people to fall through.

So it's nice to see that Senator Coburn isn't willing to play the political game, and instead is just going to demagogue the issue and scare the shit out of us so he can once again shift the tax burden from the wealthy to the needy.

Sure Senator, there are a lot of ways to fix Medicare; for example, come up with terms like "individual participation," which sound a lot better than "thinning the herd."

THE MEDICARE DEBATE
Á LA DAVID GREGORY

> "But don't we also have an obligation in government . . .
> to say to the citizens: 'You have to understand reality. Even
> though we've made a promise, there is a fiscal reality to
> this program [Medicare and Social Security] that can't be
> sustained."
> —David Gregory, corporate tool, forwarding Republican
> talking points in question form

Even high on airplane glue, I can think of three things wrong with that question.

First of all, if the government has a responsibility to explain complex issues to its citizens, then that's great—but I'm pretty sure that this would be the first time they actually did it. Also, I'm pretty sure that network news outlets—such as *Meet the Press*, you know, "your show"—have already done a pretty good job telling us all we're about to get the shaft. So the government can sit this one out.

Oh, and David, the fiscal reality actually is that Medicare *is sustainable*; what's not sustainable is the necessary political will, because corrupt lunatics have taken over the Republican party, and Democrats are a disorganized pack of nerds that keep bringing words to a gun fight.

What Gregory is suggesting is that we tell seniors, "Hey, you paid into this program your entire life—but, er, sorry." How would that be different than the U.S. defaulting on its debt? How would that be different from the U.S. failing to deliver goods and services for which payment was already received? How would that be different from the U.S. government saying, "Hey, you know that money you gave us for your doctor bills? Um, we spent it on tax cuts for the wealthy, a war in Iraq, a bank bail out . . . so, er . . . good fucking luck, man!"

AND BY THE WAY—has it not dawned on David Gregory or any of these other dimwits: What insurance company would insure today's elderly Americans, the most expensive patients in the history of the world? The fiscal reality, David, is that the Paul Ryan plan would end up taking healthcare away from seniors altogether, because the Healthcare Allowance would have nowhere to go.

Seniors without appropriate health insurance would end up wiping out huge amounts of wealth in the middle class. The estate tax would cease to be an issue—cuz there wouldn't be anyone leaving behind $2-million estates.

I don't know if the government has an obligation to say Medicare can't be fiscally sustained, but I know journalists have an obligation not to ask loaded questions based on obviously false assumptions.

ENDLESS WAR FOR ENDLESS PEACE

Q: "In how many countries are we involved in a shooting war?"
A: "That's a good question, hahahahahaha, I'll have to stop and think, hahahahaha!"
   —Secretary of Defense Leon Panetta,
      giggling through war

Like most defense secretaries, Leon Panetta lives by the credo, "If you can't enjoy invading other countries, why even get up in the morning?"

He meant no disrespect, but let's face it, explosions are funny.

You gotta see the looks on these Al Qaeda guys' faces just before the drone missile hits their SUV.

Listen, I'm not blaming Panetta for laughing—the question is incredibly simple, and the answer is ridiculously complex, like asking, "Hey, what's up Eric Cantor's ass?" There are so many things up Eric Cantor's ass. But first, Panetta might want to apologize for laughing—what with the death and whatnot. Second, it's probably a bad sign when the secretary of defense organically laughs at the question, "How many wars are we currently fighting in?"

Honestly, after his laugh, I almost expected Leon Panetta to say, "You know, now that you put it that way—I'm thinking we might have a problem."

Am I the only one that finds that fucked up? Hey, wanna have a good laugh? Think about how many countries we are fighting in while firing teachers at home? HILARIOUS!

OILY

> **"And I've said all along, the reason Dick Cheney wanted this war, it had nothing to do with WMDs or Al Qaeda or freedom and democracy, and everything to do with oil."**
> **—Col. Lawrence Wilkerson, USAF,**
> **Colin Powell's chief of staff**

Remember how everyone dismissed anyone who questioned the Official version of what happened on 9/11? Some crazy kooks, the people O'Reilly calls "loons," actually thought that the two oil men running the country just might be so oil- and money-crazy that they would start an illegal war to get more of it.

Yeah, right, I am so sick of these hippies and conspiracy nuts saying George Bush and Dick Cheney intentionally misled us into war, sure sure, nice tinfoil hats ya got there.

Well, here is Lawrence Wilkerson, retired U.S. Army colonel, and former chief of staff to U.S. Secretary of State Colin Powell, answering the question, "Just what did we get out of the Iraq war?"

"We're pretty sure there's 200 billion barrels of oil [in Iraq], maybe 300 billion. Malaki himself plans to be at 13 million barrels per day production capacity in seven years, he is already signing twenty-year contracts with Chinese and the Malaysians, covering such companies such as Exxon-Mobil, Chevron, Total, Elf, Royal Dutch, Shell, and others. He's moving out. And if these projections . . . are anything like what the geologists are telling us, this is going to be the new Saudi Arabia. So if we got anything out of this, it was the opening up of this new Saudi Arabia for the world oil markets. And I've said all along, the reason Dick Cheney wanted this war, it had nothing to do with WMDs, or Al Qaeda, or freedom and democracy, and everything to do with oil."

The last time I checked, Colonel Wilkerson was completely bald, but now he sounds like he's been growing his hair and playing hacky sack.

Here's how you start or expand a business: You develop a business plan, then you borrow money, either from a bank or from the public in the form of stocks and/or bonds.

Here's how you start the Iraq war: Sketch out a plan on a napkin, then issue as many federal bonds as you've got paper to print them on. Then lose the napkin. And, as any good business owner knows, it's fairly important to sit down and check your profit and loss reports.

Did you cover your expenses? Can you pay back your creditors? Have you built value in the business? And in the case of the Iraq war, well, let's just say, if the war was a dry cleaners, several years ago, you would have burned down that dry cleaners for the insurance money and fled the country under the alias Francisco De La

I've-never-owned-a-dry-cleaners Diego.

So, now that our business in Iraq is concluding, what did the American people get for over two trillion dollars of debt?

> **". . . right now, we're pretty sure there's 200 billion barrels of oil there, maybe 300 billion. Malaki himself plans to be at 13 million barrels per day production capacity in seven years. . . ."**

Sweet, sweet oil! Well that's totally worth it—just in terms of sheer market value, that might be better than a ten-to-one profit. Sure, you want to account for four or five thousand dead Americans, and over one hundred thousand dead Iraqis—but still, I mean we are way ahead. That's like cocaine-level profits. I bet all those assholes wouldn't have chanted "no blood for oil" if they knew just how much oil we would get back per unit of blood.

By the way, if you've seen Lawrence Wilkerson's résumé, you'll know his opinion in these matters is authoritative. If I had done just one of the things this guy has done, I would be talking about it constantly to impress girls. Back to the petroleum . . .

> **"He's already signing twenty-year contracts with the Chinese and Malaysians, covering such companies as ExxonMobil, Chevron . . . "**

Wait, Chevron?! I pump my gas there! This is going to be awesome!

> **" . . . Total, Elf, Royal Dutch, Shell, and others. He's moving out. And if these projections, and I'm sure they will be, are anything like what the geologists are telling us, this is going to be the new Saudi Arabia."**

A NEW Saudi Arabia?! Holy cow, I mean that relationship has been nothing but easy. A new Saudi Arabia is like saying a new Disneyland (where women aren't allowed to drive and most of the 9/11 hijackers were recruited).

" . . . So, if we got anything out of this, it was the opening-up of this new Saudi Arabia for the world's oil markets."

Excellent! So the oil companies will pay off America and Britain's war debt and compensate the families of all those killed in Iraq? Oh, they won't? Too bad. I just thought that would have been a nice thing to do.

". . . And I've said all along, the reason Dick Cheney wanted this war—it had nothing to do with WMDs, or Al Qaeda, or freedom and democracy, and everything to do with oil."

Uh, excuse me, but I think you meant President George W. Bush when you said Dick Cheney . . . you didn't? You meant Dick Cheney was the principal architect of the Iraq war? Well that doesn't make sense. I mean, we didn't elect that heart patient president of the United States.

The thing that slays me is here's the chief of staff to U.S. secretary of state, and he just told us in no uncertain terms that the president of the United States was cold-blooded enough to lie to his own country into starting a war, and commit multiple war crimes to accomplish it.

So, let me get this straight, these guys are rotten enough to send thousands of our sons and daughters to die in an unnecessary and illegal war, and morally bankrupt enough to use an American tragedy for monetary gain and to line the pockets of their oil buddies (and yet you're surprised when people start believing that you'd be willing to blow up two buildings in New York in the process).

So, to sum up. Next time some hippie asks you what we got for eight years, over two trillion dollars, and thousands of lives in Iraq—you say, "Oil, magical oil! What, do you think your flower bus runs on, hopes and dreams?!! No, it runs on the magic of light sweet crude—now go hide in Canada, you long-haired freak!"

LIBERTARIANS

Most people who claim to "not believe in the power of government" tend to completely rely on government all the time, but like to repeat what they hear from the corporate tool on the TV and AM radio.

If you don't believe in the power of government, then I guess you never use the water that comes out of your faucet? Or do you have a private company that takes care of that?

And you never drive on a highway, right? Or the road in front of your house? Or are you one of those rotten deadbeats who relies on the government to build roads for them?

And I bet you never flush your toilet either, right? Or are you one of those freeloaders who uses the government's sewers?

And you never throw garbage out either, right? You burn it in your backyard, correct? Or do you rely on the government to come and take *all* of your garbage away every day?

And I bet when the guy from the government shows up at your door every day with mail, you tell him to "Get lost!" cuz you are a rugged individualist who doesn't need welfare; you can deliver your own mail! That's what you say, right?

And I bet you never use the police, either. Only people who need the government to protect them call the police; the rest of us call Mannix!

Same thing when your house catches fire—you're not gonna sit around and wait for the government to show up and put it out with their filthy government firemen, are you? Of course not, you get your garden hose out that is hooked up to your own private water source and put it out by yourself, right?

And you never eat food from the grocery store either, right? Cuz the government makes sure that the food we eat isn't poisoned and safe to eat, but you don't eat that food, right?

And I bet you never got educated at a public school, right? Or went to a public university? Cuz that is socialism. You don't need the government to educate you, leave that up to the corporations; they will tell us everything we need to know.

And you probably have never taken a trip on an airplane, right? Or a train? Or been to a public park? Or a public library? Or taken a prescription drug?

Now how 'bout my favorite, say it with me: "Keep your government hands off my Medicare!"

What's really happening with this type of person is they imagine the government is helping someone else, who might even be a different race from themselves. They resent the taxes they pay that might help people who are worse off than themselves. They live in a Social Darwinist fantasy where they succeeded in life separate from the society they live in, looking down with contempt on their fellow citizens.

It is very disheartening to see that, in the middle of getting the biggest reaming ever from Wall Street and the military industrial complex, some people still reserve the bulk of their scorn and anger for the poorest in society. Yeah, it's the people with no money and no power who crashed our economy, laid off our teachers, and kicked people out of their houses. That's it. Let's get those greedy bastards at the bottom! Ugh.

THE SURVEILLANCE STATE:
IT'S FOR YOUR OWN GOOD

> "I'm not for profiling people on the color of their skin or their religion, but I would have to take into account where they've been traveling, and perhaps you might have to indirectly take into account whether or not they've been going to radical political speeches by religious leaders, but it wouldn't be that they are Islamic. But if someone is attending speeches from someone who is promoting the violent overthrow of our government, that's really an offense we should be going after; they should be deported or put in prison."
> —Rand Paul, scaring the shit out of me

Did you catch that? He's not for profiling Muslims necessarily, but if you are *around someone* who is saying some *bad stuff*, you can go to jail. So I guess he's all for free speech, just not *free listening*.

When students and pregnant women were being pepper sprayed at Occupy Wall Street protests, TV talking heads were falling over themselves to defend these attacks. These were the same pundits that defended gun brandishing Teabaggers who were basically protesting the president being black.

PRE-OCCUPIED

Do you remember the Occupy Wall Street demonstration at UC Davis back in November of 2011? It stirred up the press everywhere but their conscience.

"A video has gone viral of peaceful students being pepper sprayed on the UC Davis campus is raising the question: Is law enforcement going over the line in dealing with protests?"
—Ed Schultz, MSNBC

Next question: "Cancer, is it really that bad for you?"

PEPPER IS FOOD

When students and pregnant women were being pepper-sprayed at Occupy Wall Street protests, TV talking heads were falling over themselves to defend those attacks. These were the same pundits that defended gun-brandishing Teabaggers who were basically protesting the president being black. Bill O'Reilly and Megyn Blonde WOWman confer:

Bilbo: "First of all, pepper spray just burns your eyes, right?"
Blonde: "It's a derivative of actual pepper; it's a food product, essentially."

Yes, and lead bullets are really just fat pencils, essentially. And billy clubs are really just tickle sticks.

Over at Fox Business News, someone advocates for peace:

"Reminder to those who disagree with those they find disagreeable—hear 'em, don't gas 'em, because every time you do you cede the advantage to them . . ."
—Neil Cavuto

Yeah, don't beat the protesters. Not cuz it is horrible and goes against everything we claim to believe in in America. Don't beat them cuz, when we do, we lose the support of people we can usually trick into supporting us. You have to read between the lines, but yes, he is still being a douchebag.

What Neil is telling his fellow free-speech-hating conservatives is they've made this mistake before, when police overreacted with fire hoses and guns, and the result was black people got to eat at the same restaurants as whites. And he wants to make sure something like that never happens again.

Remember, the goal is always ignore the people protesting, unless they're protesting against Obamacare.

> **"A lot of these folks who think that somehow money grows on trees and they're entitled to it and they don't understand how wealth is produced in this country."**
> **—Senator Jon Kyl, on Occupy Wall Street**

See these OWS types don't know how to produce wealth; they think you work hard and save and then you have a good life. These people are idiots living in a fantasyland known as "the past."

Today, anyone with half a brain knows that the way you produce wealth is through outsourcing jobs to slave labor to cut costs and raise profits, and also through crony capitalism funded by trillions in taxpayer-funded subsidies from a corrupt, bought government.

> **"What have we seen here: violence, rape, arson, destruction of property, sex in public, masturbation in public, naked people, drugs, drug paraphernalia, anti-Americanism, anti-Semitism, anti-capitalism."**
> **—Sean Hannity, on OWS**

Um Sean, you forgot to add . . . nope, you got 'em all.

One question: Is that his complaints about the OWS or just the list of the stuff Sean jerked off to today?

But of course Hannity makes Occupy Wall Street seem like a lot more fun than it really is.

I guess what he's saying is that there's nothing more disgusting than a bunch of dirty, degenerate protesters making a completely valid point.

> **"It starts with a premise that we all owe them everything; they take over a public park they didn't pay for, to go nearby to use bathrooms they didn't pay for, to beg for food from places they don't want to pay for, to obstruct those who are going to work to pay the taxes to sustain the bathrooms and the park . . . . You need to reassert something as simple as saying to them, 'Go get a job right after you take a bath.'"**
> **—Newt Gingrich, on OWS**

To the people unable to find employment in a depression, Wall Street lobbyist and crack-up Newt Gingrich says, "Get a job." Oh boy Newt, that is a funny one, seeing as your job was making sure that the people who ruined the economy and rigged the game so that they received taxpayer-funded welfare when they went bankrupt, and everyone else lost their jobs, houses, and retirement. Hella funny, Newt!

Not quite as hilarious as the time you punk'd your wife by serving her divorce papers in front of your kids in the hospital room where she was recovering from cancer surgery. Not that funny, but still right up there.

All his experience in Congress, and it turns out that Newt has the same understanding of our economy as Herman Cain.

What the protesters want is basic fairness in our economy, but Newt decides to smear them and say that these protesters want everything for nothing, and he's gonna make sure they're not gonna get it, mostly because we already gave it to the banks.

I guess I see his point; these people need to pick themselves up by their bootstraps, roll up their sleeves, and become lobbyists. I mean, why are we listening to the economic complaints of a bunch of people who don't even have jobs? And why don't they have jobs? Because these protesters are so lazy, they've stopped looking for jobs, just because there aren't any.

And let's not forget the worst thing about these hippies; they don't even pay taxes! Who do they think they are, General Electric?

Their mistake is asking for a living wage instead of a billion-dollar parachute.

Lou Dobbs has a show on the Fox Business channel. Who knew? You mean, besides the over two dozen regular viewers, I've heard estimates that almost half of all the people working at Fox Business channel know.

Well here he is, talking with political strategist Dick Morris. Let's remember that Morris was the advisor who helped President Clinton make the difficult transition from Democrat to Republican. He was born Richard Morris, yet freely chose the name Dick. And to prove that he is, Dick made the following comparison:

> **"When you get a leftist movement like this going on that goes way over, it puts the president in a very, very difficult situation. Just think of the flip side, if you had a large Klan movement in the United States with a Republican president."**
> **—Dick Morris, right wing pollster/horrible person**

"Just think if we had a large Klan movement with a Republican president?"

Don't we always?

First: Occupy Wall Street = the Klan? WTF? Sure, that works, because demonstrating against corporate greed and corruption is equivalent to racism.

Second: What the fuck? So, apparently, the rich were brought over here in trust fund boats 400 years ago to slave in our nation's investment firm belt? Separated from their Krugerands. Families torn apart. One brother forced to sell derivatives at Goldman Sachs, the other cheating senior citizens at Lehman Brothers. Heartbreaking. Then after the "War Between the Banks," the OWS movement forms, ushering in a series of repressive anti-Ponzi laws. And for over 100 years, poor bankers all over the country live in mini-apartheids, wondering where their next opportunity to siphon some retiree's pension fund will come from. They must be terror-stricken.

Third: Lou Dobbs has to start drinking again.

Fourth: There is a large Klan movement, it's called the Tea Party.

"I understand the frustrations that are being expressed in those protests; in some ways, they're not that much different from some of the protests we saw coming from the Tea Party, both on the Left and the Right, people feel separated from their government, that their institutions aren't looking out for them."
—President Obama, on OWS

Oh yeah, he's down with OWS, and they're totally just like the Tea Party, you know, except for the fact that they are informed, right on the issues and not being co-opted by puppets of the very institutions they are protesting against. Except for that, they are a lot alike. The OWS protestors and the Tea Party are exactly alike, except the OWS protestor votes correctly, and the Tea Party has not only been duped into voting against their own interests, but this time they are also protesting and organizing against their own interests, too. So, yeah, except for that, they are a lot alike.

"So the Occupy Wall Street movement is dead, finished as a legitimate political force in this country, and that's a good thing."
 —Bill O'Reilly, on OWS

So that's good, and I guess everything's settled now. Next!

THOSE BLOODSUCKING TEACHERS

"What we need to be talking about is not hiring more teachers but hiring better teachers, and getting rid of the ones that don't teach. When 50% of the kids in Chicago aren't even graduating, we need to be talking about improving education, not use increasing the number of public employees, who in Chicago get over $100,000 in salary."
 —Rev. Mike Huckabee, demonizing teachers

We need to shit on teachers and pay them less because Chicago has a 50% dropout rate? How is a 50% dropout rate the fault of the teachers?

Half the kids don't show up to school, and it's the teacher's fault for not teaching them?

If most people in a neighborhood have dirty cars because they don't take their cars in to get washed, it's not the fault of the guys who work at the car wash, is it?

How do we hire better-quality teachers when you don't want to pay them and want to make it less attractive to be a teacher in the first place?

Chicago teachers earn $74,000 a year. So Huckabee throws out the $100,000 number to get other working people angry at teachers.

Of course George Snuffleupagus isn't aware of the pertinent facts of the situation, nor does he seem familiar with the bogus talking points of the corporate mouthpiece Mike Huckabee.

If Chicago public school teachers made $100,000 a year, there would be a line all the way to Florida for people applying to teaching schools.

Nobody brings up class size. Huckabee says we don't need to hire more teachers, but class size makes a big difference in student achievement.

Tennessee's Project STAR (Student Teacher Achievement Ratio) found that smaller class sizes had positive effects at every grade level across all locations, from rural to urban. It also was superior on every achievement measure and for all subjects, from reading to mathematics to the sciences. Students in early grades assigned to small classes of 15 or so, graduate on schedule at higher rates (76%) compared to students from regular classes of over 24 (64%). These same students complete school with honors and drop out of school less often compared to those who go to regular classes.

"Teachers and firefighters aren't private sector jobs; they don't contribute to economic growth."
—Rush Limbaugh

So according to our favorite college dropout/economist, teachers aren't real workers, and they are not a part of the economy.

Let me get this straight: When a teacher gets paid, they spend that money in an alternate universe, not in the communities and cities where they live, but somewhere else where the money doesn't go into the economy.

Again, this is why you don't take lessons on how the economy works from a college dropout.

BECKEL UP!

When you're a supposed liberal that works for Fox News, it does not speak well of you, both as a liberal and as a human being. Cuz Fox News hires two kinds of liberals, either:

A) Alan Colmes—a weenie who makes liberal positions look weeniesh; or

B) Bob Beckel—a guy who's basically not a liberal.

"I'm a strong union supporter, and a strong supporter of the teachers unions. However, having said that . . . "
—Bob Beckel, feeble liberal

See, now this is the kind of preamble that is precisely akin to people who say they are not racist just before they say something incredibly racist.

FYI: If you're such a strong supporter of the unions, maybe you should try, just a little, to see things from their point of view. Like when they say means testing is not working, and they're willing to go out on strike over it, maybe you ask why.

Here's an idea: Why not have a teacher on your little show to explain their point of view? Just saying, "news" is in the title of your network, and not "bloviating idiot giving his opinion about stuff he doesn't really understand."

"For a long time I've supported means testing for teachers."

What?! A means test is a test of how much money a dude has—to see if he's poor enough to get some dough. Are we gonna do that with teachers? Cuz according to the Republican machine, teachers have sacks and sacks of jewels and cash. They're not going to qualify.

I'm pretty sure what he meant to say was some sort of standard-ized performance testing for teachers. Yeah, in the unbelievably complex and humanly flawed quest to teach an ever-changing population of children from drastically different regions of the country—how could a standardized test go awry?

"They want these people who've been let go of the school system to automatically come back."

Outrageous! The teachers unions want people who were laid off for financial reasons to be the first reinstated? What the fuck? I mean, you'd think that was how a layoff works or something.

"The reason they're out is because they weren't good teachers."

I have no reason to believe this is actually why they were retired, but I'm gonna say it anyway, cuz that's just how I roll.

"So the idea that they should be the first in line to get teaching jobs is crazy."

And even though the premise of this conclusion is a house of cards, I'm pretty sure the conclusion is totally solid.

"And by the way, the 35%—they moved immediately off of that. It wasn't about the pay increase, cuz they knew they weren't gonna get that much—"

Just thought I'd totally gloss over that fact—that the teachers are not striking about money, like the greedy fat cats Fox News would have you believe they are.

"But they're holding up on this issue about teachers should be rated on what their kids do on these standardized tests. Why not?"

Good question, why don't you actually ask someone who actually works in education? Is it because they might actually have a reason that makes sense? Yes, that would drag your whole show to a screeching halt, wouldn't it?

By the way, I'm not a highly paid political pundit and professor of politics at a major university like Bob here, but it turns out there's this thing called Google, where you can actually look up the arguments against national standardized testing and evaluating teachers based on that testing. It seems, and this is crazy if you ask me, their main objection is that it doesn't work.

AMERICA, I CAN'T QUIT YOU

> "Government by organized money is just as dangerous as government by organized mob."
> —Franklin Delano Roosevelt

The country is no longer what it claims to be—a nation of hope and prosperity for all, a nation with Justice For All. The problem is the same as it has always been: Money flows upward and gets concentrated, corrupting everything, while leaving the majority behind. We've let the bastards take control again. The bastards being organized money. As FDR said:

> "The liberty of a democracy is not safe if the people tolerate the growth of private power to a point where it becomes stronger than their democratic state itself. That, in its essence, is fascism—ownership of government by an individual, by a group.
>   "We had to struggle with the old enemies of peace—business and financial monopoly, speculation, reckless banking, class antagonism, sectionalism, war profiteering. They had begun to consider the government of the United States as a mere appendage to their own affairs. We know now that government by organized money is just as dangerous as government by organized mob. Never before in all our history have these forces been so united against one candidate as they stand today. They are unanimous in their hate for me—and I welcome their hatred."

We now have Republicans and Democrats ignoring Roosevelt's wisdom and have effectively repealed the New Deal. We are right back to the same place we were in 1936. The difference is that, back then, we had FDR to push back against the bastards, now we have someone pushing with the bastards.

Barack Obama does not, nor do many Democrats, "welcome their hate." In fact, most of them fear their hate because they "welcome their money" in the form of campaign donations.

And that's the problem: The plutocrats have effectively gamed the system by BUYING IT and rewriting the rules to serve themselves. Which is why we are now living in a new Gilded Age. Remember that Mark Twain referred to the Gilded Age as a time when serious social problems were hidden by a "thin gold gilding."

The antidote for these problems should be the Fourth Estate—the supposed watchdogs of our society. Our free press is so important, it is one of only three professions mentioned in the Constitution.

But there aren't any watchdogs anymore because they put them in the kennel. Not all at once, but slowly and very deliberately. CEOs of corporations and the heads of banks (aka criminals) have always bought our politicians to help get the rules rigged in their favor.

It used to be the role of the Fourth Estate to monitor our politicians and their donators. But the criminals got smart and decided to buy the watchdog, too.

Now there is nobody watching the store, and the dog has been hired by the very criminals they are supposed to be watching.

They've even made a mockery of the judicial system. Remember the last time a candidate with fewer votes was appointed president by the Supreme Court?

Justice Stevens wrote a scathing dissent on the Court's ruling to stay the recount of votes in Florida during the 2000 presidential election. He believed that the holding displayed:

"an unstated lack of confidence in the impartiality and capacity of the state judges who would make the critical decisions if the vote count were to proceed.

"The endorsement of that position by the majority of this Court can only lend credence to the most cynical appraisal

of the work of judges throughout the land. It is confidence in the men and women who administer the judicial system that is the true backbone of the rule of law. Time will one day heal the wound to that confidence that will be inflicted by today's decision. One thing, however, is certain. Although we may never know with complete certainty the identity of the winner of this year's presidential election, the identity of the loser is perfectly clear. It is the Nation's confidence in the judge as an impartial guardian of the rule of law."

And that is the same court that went on to rule in the Citizens United case, which decided that corporations can spend as much corporate money on political campaigns as they want, revealing that the true owners of the country are the ones with the most money. They now spend the cash to get their puppet elected, and then the puppet votes to give them even more power and rigs the game even more in the plutocrats' favor.

This isn't news to anyone; it's just information that never gets discussed when and where it should be being discussed . . . which is all the time, everywhere.

We are living with the consequences of these decisions now. We are now seeing the biggest income disparity in our country since the Gilded Age. Corporate profits are back to record highs, and the banks are bigger and richer than ever, thanks to the taxpayers. And yet most Americans are barely treading water in the richest country in the world.

It's the corporatization of our entire culture. We have let unbridled, unregulated capitalism become religious dogma that never gets questioned. We are now privatizing everything, including education.

We are constantly being told (by the paid tools in the corporate media) that teachers are really the greedy ones in our culture, and they are lazy and your kid would be getting a better education if we just let a corporation do it.

What that means is privatizing education, taking it from being a state service with professional workers dedicated to education and giving it to private corporations who are dedicated to turning a profit.

And the data is in: They don't work. Four out of five charter schools perform neither better nor worse than the public schools they want to replace. And that's after they broken the teachers union, gotten rid of the most experienced teachers, and discouraged other quality people from entering the profession, because we now have a system that views teachers as "the problem."

The way out of this is going to have to come from us, from our organizing, from massive protests like Occupy Wall Street, and from enough people raising their voices.

America is progressive.

Americans are progressive.

Most of us believe in a fair playing field for all, and that everybody who works should share in our increased prosperity. Most Americans embrace modern-day Liberalism. How do I know that? That's what they were voting for when they voted for Barack Obama, who very cleverly campaigns as a populist and a liberal. Unfortunately, he quickly disowned that ideology when in power, enjoying hanging out with the likes of Larry Summers and Robert Rubin.

The only solution is the obvious one: We need to turn the country back over to the people and the people who are responsive to the people. The only way to do that is: Get the money out of politics.

We can't do anything until we get that done. Ironically, it appears that we need to raise a shit ton of money to do that.

P.S.
AMERICA,
I LOVE YOU!

What do I love about America? Well, it's got less Indians in it than it used to. That's a joke. I guess what makes me hopeful for America is that we had those yearning to be free, who took the gamble of a better future, and the founding fathers who risked their lives to sign a Declaration of Independence, which states that . . .

"We hold these truths to be self-evident, that all men are created equal, that they are endowed by their Creator with certain unalienable Rights, that among these are Life, Liberty and the pursuit of Happiness. That to secure these rights, Governments are instituted among Men, deriving their just powers from the consent of the governed, that whenever any Form of Government becomes destructive of these ends, it is the Right of the People to alter or to abolish it, and institute a new Government."

That right there continues to give me hope for the future of America. Men wrote those ideas over 200 years ago; it was a radical departure from what came before it, which was a king or queen and their inbred children.

We are a nation of immigrants, and it has created a hybrid culture that is truly remarkable. If we remember what American Exceptionalism really means: that the U.S. is qualitatively different from other nations because of a uniquely American ideology based on liberty, egalitarianism, individualism, republicanism, and populism.

I love this country because of its rich history of standing up for the little guy in the face of the big guy. That we eventually get things right, even if it takes a while.

We still have that Declaration of Independence and the Constitution! And yes, I'm re-appropriating the Constitution from Right-Wingers who use it for cheap emotional effect but probably haven't read it.

Just think of the Bill of Rights! We take too many of those rights for granted. Of course, not the second one; everybody knows we have to stay vigilant about the Second Amendment because, if we don't, it will lose industrialists' money, specifically gun manufacturers' money, so they spend a lot of money reminding everybody how important it is.

Boy, imagine if we could invent a gun that shot nothing but Fourth Amendment protections. But that is getting us back to what is wrong with this country.

"There is nothing wrong with America that can't be fixed by what is right with America."
–Bill Clinton, impeached

We have an immigration problem, and who better to fix that problem than a nation of immigrants?

We have a financial crisis, and what better to lead us out of it than being the richest country in the world?

I think it's great that we share this North American continent with Mexico and Canada, yet we are the only ones who call ourselves "Americans," and so does everyone else. I don't know if that is hubris or just because it would sound stupid calling ourselves "United States-ens" or "United State-ers."

Plus, don't overlook the reason we will always be the greatest nation in history, and that is because we saved the world from Fascism and Communism. There is no mistaking that. So that will remain forever a big deal; we saved the world from the Nazis and went to the moon. Those are super big things. And we did them, because America is, at its best, the best of humanity.

And we continue to get better; we continue to go forward and not backward. The nation has gone from bombing black churches to electing a black president within two generations.

And we have Silicon Valley and the two biggest computer giants, Bill Gates and the late Steve Jobs—their products have enriched and annoyed our lives beyond measure. Americans dream the future.

We still have the FDA and the EPA and FEMA and Social Security and Medicare and Medicaid. We still do lots of great progressive things. We just passed the Affordable Healthcare Act. We did it. It's flawed and not the right fix, but it is a step in the right direction. The point is, we keep going forward, not backward, getting better not worse. The problem is not the people of America, but when ruling institutions work for the moneyed elite and lose touch with the people.

With all that is at stake in this country, we have had the peaceful transfer of power now for over two centuries. As we look around the world, we realize that's something. Forgive me for sounding like Sarah Palin, but "golly gee!" Egypt didn't last through one term before the military ended their democratic experiment. We have somehow managed 230 years of peaceful transfers of power; that's 43 times, we have remained committed to that principle.

And the country is becoming more liberal and more progressive every day. We are still filling up this country with immigrants, which, if history is any guide, can only be a good thing for America.

Yes, there are still a few death rattles of darker days that surface from time to time—minority voter suppression, race baiting, the banks that are "too big to fail" that continue to extract wealth from this country, but we are moving forward and will get better.

Plus we have better restaurants than most other places. Let's just start with New York and San Francisco, which to the foodie, appear to be cities set up just so we could eat at their amazing restaurants. San Francisco alone boasts of 23 Michelin stars awarded inside the city limits; that's 2.9 stars per 100,000 people. As Ron Paul would say, "Not too shabby." And Manhattan does even better by posting 4.2 Michelin stars per 100,000 people. Sure, it's no Lyon, France, or Bergamo, Italy, but if it were, there would be absolutely no reason to go to those places.

America produced Bruce Springsteen. If that was our only contribution to the music scene, we could hold our head high, but it doesn't even scratch the surface. Americans don't just play music, we invent music. Americans invented Jazz and Blues and hip-hop! Let that knowledge fester in the pride pod! We produced Louis Armstrong, Frank Sinatra . . . THE BEATLES!

We invented stand-up comedy, which up until very recently was strictly an American phenomenon. Think about that—there are plenty of other countries with no stand-up comedians.

How sad for an entire nation to go through life not knowing how horrible their airline food is and how different guys are from women. But we don't have to worry about that because we are AMERICANS and we have Bob Hope, Jerry Seinfeld, George Carlin, Bill Hicks.

How about *Hollywood* in general? Our entertainment industry is the envy of the world, what other country could boast that they are currently funding and producing *Fast & Furious 8*!? That's right, NONE. George Clooney didn't move to Canada to make it in movies, but Michael J. Fox moved to America, didn't he?

And we still try to solve problems around the world; we have a genuine commitment to humanitarian efforts around the globe. Even the warmonger George Bush turned heads with his AIDS initiative in Africa. Have you ever heard of the Russian Aids Initiative? Didn't think so.

What else can I tell you about my country that hasn't been said already? The best thing about this country is that I am allowed to write this book that criticizes all the corrupt people who own and run the country. We really do have freedom of speech, which not even Canada has. Betcha' didn't know that, aye?

Bottom line is that the majority of Americans still believe in the very progressive ideals this country was founded on, and that will fix all of our problems. We have freedom, we have liberty, we might have to constantly fight to safeguard them from tyrants, but we have them, and we have a commitment to them on paper in the form of the Constitution.

And that is why we have people like Private Bradley Manning and Edward Snowden, who are willing to risk everything so that our country can be better, can live up to its ideals, so the American people will know what its government does in the dark.

If you've ever read Private Manning's letter to President Obama, you know the kind of patriot he is and how badly we need him and more like him. If you've never read it, then I will include it for you here. Read this, and tell me this guy is an enemy of America:

> "The decisions that I made in 2010 were made out of a concern for my country and the world that we live in. Since the tragic events of 9/11, our country has been at war. We've been at war with an enemy that chooses not to meet us on any traditional battlefield, and due to this fact, we've had to alter our methods of combating the risks posed to us and our way of life.
>
> "I initially agreed with these methods and chose to volunteer to help defend my country. It was not until I was in Iraq and reading secret military reports on a daily basis that I started to question the morality of what we were doing.
>
> "It was at this time I realized that (in) our efforts to meet the risk posed to us by the enemy, we have forgotten our humanity.
>
> "We consciously elected to devalue human life both in

Iraq and Afghanistan. When we engaged those that we perceived were the enemy, we sometimes killed innocent civilians. Whenever we killed innocent civilians, instead of accepting responsibility for our conduct, we elected to hide behind the veil of national security and classified information in order to avoid any public accountability.

"In our zeal to kill the enemy, we internally debated the definition of torture. We held individuals at Guantanamo for years without due process. We inexplicably turned a blind eye to torture and executions by the Iraqi government. And we stomached countless other acts in the name of our war on terror.

"Patriotism is often the cry extolled when morally questionable acts are advocated by those in power. When these cries of patriotism drown out any logically based dissension, it is usually the American soldier that is given the order to carry out some ill-conceived mission.

"Our nation has had similar dark moments for the virtues of democracy—the Trail of Tears, the Dred Scott decision, McCarthyism, and the Japanese-American internment camps—to mention a few. I am confident that many of the actions since 9/11 will one day be viewed in a similar light.

"As the late Howard Zinn once said, 'There is not a flag large enough to cover the shame of killing innocent people.'

"I understand that my actions violated the law; I regret if my actions hurt anyone or harmed the United States. It was never my intent to hurt anyone. I only wanted to help people. When I chose to disclose classified information, I did so out of a love for my country and a sense of duty to others.

"If you deny my request for a pardon, I will serve my time knowing that sometimes you have to pay a heavy price to live in a free society.

"I will gladly pay that price if it means we could have a country that is truly conceived in liberty and dedicated to the proposition that all women and men are created equal."

Now if you are like me, that letter surpassed anything I ever thought he would say, and it made me choke up a little. The guy my country tortured is a super patriot, who knew?

My pride for my country comes from the Occupy Wall Street protesters who did the most American thing you can do: protest in the streets. It's the Philadelphia Police captain who put on his uniform and joined the OWS protesters because he realized he is them and not the corporation who bought the politician who ordered him to knock his fellow citizen's head in.

I get pride from our supposed Public Enemy #1, Edward Snowden. If the news reports are to be believed, this little anti-American asshole is nothing more than a creep with a narcissistic personality disorder . . . this being said by grown men who put on make-up and sit in front of a camera for a living.

In the words and deeds of Private Manning and Edward Snowden, I feel the same spirit that inspired the Founding Fathers to write the Bill of Rights.

"You can't come forward against the world's most powerful intelligence agencies and be completely free from risk, because they're such powerful adversaries that no one can meaningfully oppose them. If they want to get you, they'll get you in time. But at the same time, you have to make a determination about what it is that's important to you.

And if living—living comfortably but less free is something you're willing to accept—and I think many of us are; it's the human nature—you can get up every day, go to work, collect your large paycheck for relatively little toil, labor against the public interest, and go to sleep at night after watching your shows.

"But if you realize that that's the world that you helped create, and it's going to get worse with the next generation and the next generation, who extend the capabilities of this sort of architecture of oppression, you realize that you might be willing to accept any risk, and it doesn't matter what the outcome is, so long as the public gets to make their own decisions about how that's applied."

These are the Americans who are willing to give up all that America has to offer in order to make it better. These are the Americans that will make the future better. They have always been here throughout its history. That's the America I know. That's the America I love.

ACKNOWLEDGMENTS

This book is the culmination of 25 years as a professional comedian. Comedy is the most singular thing I can think of doing for a living, yet I could not have done it without the help of many generous and talented people. I thank the following people for their inspiration, encouragement, accommodation, and love.

My wife Stef Zamorano, I am indebted to her for so many things, not the least of which is the support and encouragement she gave me throughout this entire process. She is my right hand, my other self, and the best wife in the world.

My manager Alex Murray, who continues to make my dreams come true. While others doubted me, he expected me to succeed and showed me how to think big. This book is a tribute to his mindset.

This book is an outgrowth of doing a satirical news show for KPFK radio in Los Angeles. That show is the result of the courage, sharp eyes, and hard work of Ali Lexa and Alan Minsky.

Every week on The Jimmy Dore Show, I have the amazing good fortune to work with some of the brightest minds in comedy. Robert Yasumura, a brilliantly funny writer with a wonderful imagination and an amazing gift for perfectly framing complicated issues. His humor and help with this project was instrumental, I will forever be grateful.

Steve Rosenfield packs a lot of humanity into his sardonic sense of humor. He writes the greatest one-liners since Henny Youngman and has the ability to pillory the world's biggest douchebags with one sentence.

Frank Conniff, a true comedy savant, the most quick-witted comedian around, who speaks in perfectly formed jokes and raises puns to high art. Eliciting a laugh from Frank will always be the highest compliment a joke can receive.

The brilliantly funny Marc Van Landuyt, his writing is not only hilarious, but he takes down targets with pin point accuracy. His insight, guidance, and constant hand-holding were integral to the making of this book. He is always a pure delight, his outrages are as entertaining as his joys. I wish everyone a friend like Marc.

Mike MacRae is the funniest impressionist who ever lived. That is not an overstatement. Not only does he capture people's voices, but by some unexplainable voodoo, captures a piece of their dark souls as well. He makes comedy work a pure joy.

Jim Earl, who is so funny he makes us laugh at death on a regular basis. His sketches and jokes are always a welcomed treat.

Paul Gilmartin for lending his talent and making his outrage a highpoint of the show. And my sincerest gratitude goes to all the writers and performers who have made The Jimmy Dore Show possible, I am truly indebted and proud to know you all.

The friend who literally drove me to Los Angeles on January 1st 1995 was John Bongiorno. He then drove to New York and stayed, and I have missed him ever since.

Ben Mankiewicz- who had nothing to do with the writing of this book, and when I say nothing, I mean zero. But his friendship, humor, and masterful telling of the greatest Hollywood stories of all time, were around when I needed it.

Guys like Cenk Uygar make guys like me possible. You can find inspiration in many places but none better than the life and career of Cenk Uygar. He has made a life out of doing things others said could not be done. The Young Turks is the future of media, which assures that the future is bright.

Steve Oh, for his support and friendship, for having a first rate sense of humor, and for putting The Jimmy Dore Show in front of cameras. My never ending gratitude to Tom Hank and Hank Thompson for introducing me to The Young Turks.

Anna Kasparian, Dave Kohler, Irina Nichita, Jesus Godoy, Jayar Jackson, Johnny Iadarola, Dave Rubin, Edwin Umana, Tim Collins and everyone at TYT who make it such a great place.

My deepest gratitude goes to the hilarious and supremely talented Patton Oswalt, for letting people know that he listens to The Jimmy Dore show. His magnanimous help in spreading the word about the show has been invaluable.

Thanks to the best improv-er's in the world—Matt Besser, Matt Walsh, Seth Morris, and everyone at the UCB Theater, for giving me the opportunity to do my own show. It was a very generous offer that ended up being a turning point in my career as I discovered what I really wanted to talk about.

My editor Jennifer Kasius and everyone at Running Press for believing in the book and making this dream happen.

And thanks to Donkey Hotey, for classing up the book with his wonderful artwork. I am a huge fan and beyond thrilled he was able to work on this project.

Andi Smith, for being the best person to bounce ideas off of and for always making me scream with laughter.

Tadzio Wellisz and Carolyn Feruzzi for their love and support always, and for making sure I was well fed to the point of being out of my mind throughout this process.

Special thanks to my brothers Tony and Miles for their humor, support, and love. They were my first comedy teachers and the laughs we shared are forever treasured.

Nothing made me grow as a performer more than doing The Marijuana-logues with three hilarious and wonderfully generous comedians, Doug Benson, Tony Camin, and Arj Barker. I am forever thankful for being part of something so great as a hit Off-Broadway show.

I will always remember the much needed helping hand and fantastic opportunities afforded to me by the lovely Lisa Leingang. Thank you for helping make my early years in LA so fun and worthwhile.

Tom Griswold, a man at the top of his profession who did not have to make time for me, but did anyway. Thank you for your incredible support when I most needed it, and for the most generous gift of producing my first cd.

To the fine folks who so graciously invited me on their stages and television shows and let me tell my jokes. From the bottom of my heart, THANK YOU! Jamie Flam, Roger Feeney, Burt Haas, Cyndi Nelson, Burt Borth, Mike Kurtz, Dave Dennison, Richard Barrett, Mike Lacey, Dave Reinitz, Barbara Holliday, Jamie Masada,Ron Lynch, Paul Kozlowski, Matt Behrens, Matt Chavez, Joaquin Trujillo, Molly Schminke, Lisa Young, Don Learned, Heather Woodhull, Dee Burdett, Cliff Diedrich,Erin Pooler-von Schonfeldt, Bob Fisher, Andrew Unger, Andy Wood, Chick & Patty, Linda Turk, Zoe Friedman, Dave Rath, Bart Coleman, Marshall Chiles, Colleen Quinn, Bud Friedman, Flannigan.

I have no idea how anyone gets through life without the companionship of a dog. I have been blessed to have experienced the love of Bubba and Brownie, the sweetest and most gentle souls I have ever known. To god's most perfect creatures, thank you.

As hard as it may be to believe, this is only a pa rtial list of all the many generous souls who lent a helping hand to me along my journey. To all those friends who I met in comedy clubs and morning radio shows across the nation, thank you!

PHOTO CREDITS

ILLUSTRATION CREDITS

29, 210: Bill_OReilly_Caricature DonkeyHotey/Flickr, World Affairs Council
of Philadelphia

32: Luke_Russert_Caricature DonkeyHotey/Flickr, Megan Robertson,
U.S. House, US Capitol

37, 73: Tom_Brokaw_Caricature DonkeyHotey/Flickr, Wikimedia,
U.S. Defense Department, U.S. Air Force

78: John_Boehner_Caricature DonkeyHotey/Flickr, Mark Taylor

87: Rick_Santorum_Caricature DonkeyHotey/Flickr, Gage Skidmore

90: Chris_Christie_Caricature DonkeyHotey/Flickr, Bob Jagendorf

108: Michael_Bloomberg_Caricature DonkeyHotey/Flickr,
U.S. Defense Department

134: George_Bush_Caricature DonkeyHotey/Flickr, U.S. Air Force

141, 160: Barack_Obama_Caricature DonkeyHotey/Flickr, Whitehouse